Montana Animal Coloring Book

Copyrighted Material

All Rights Reserved By

Monica Mountain

Grizzly Bear

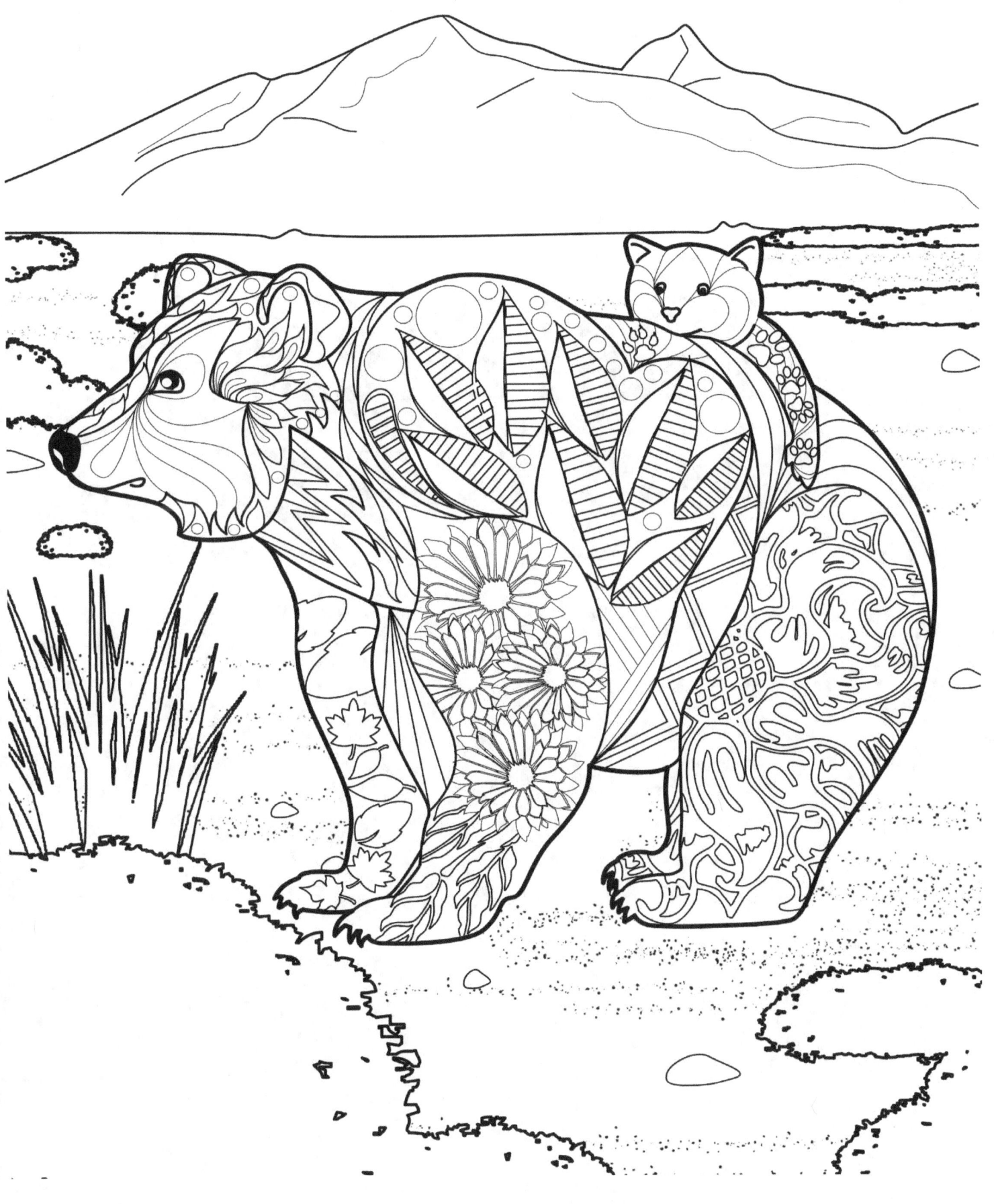

Bald Eagle

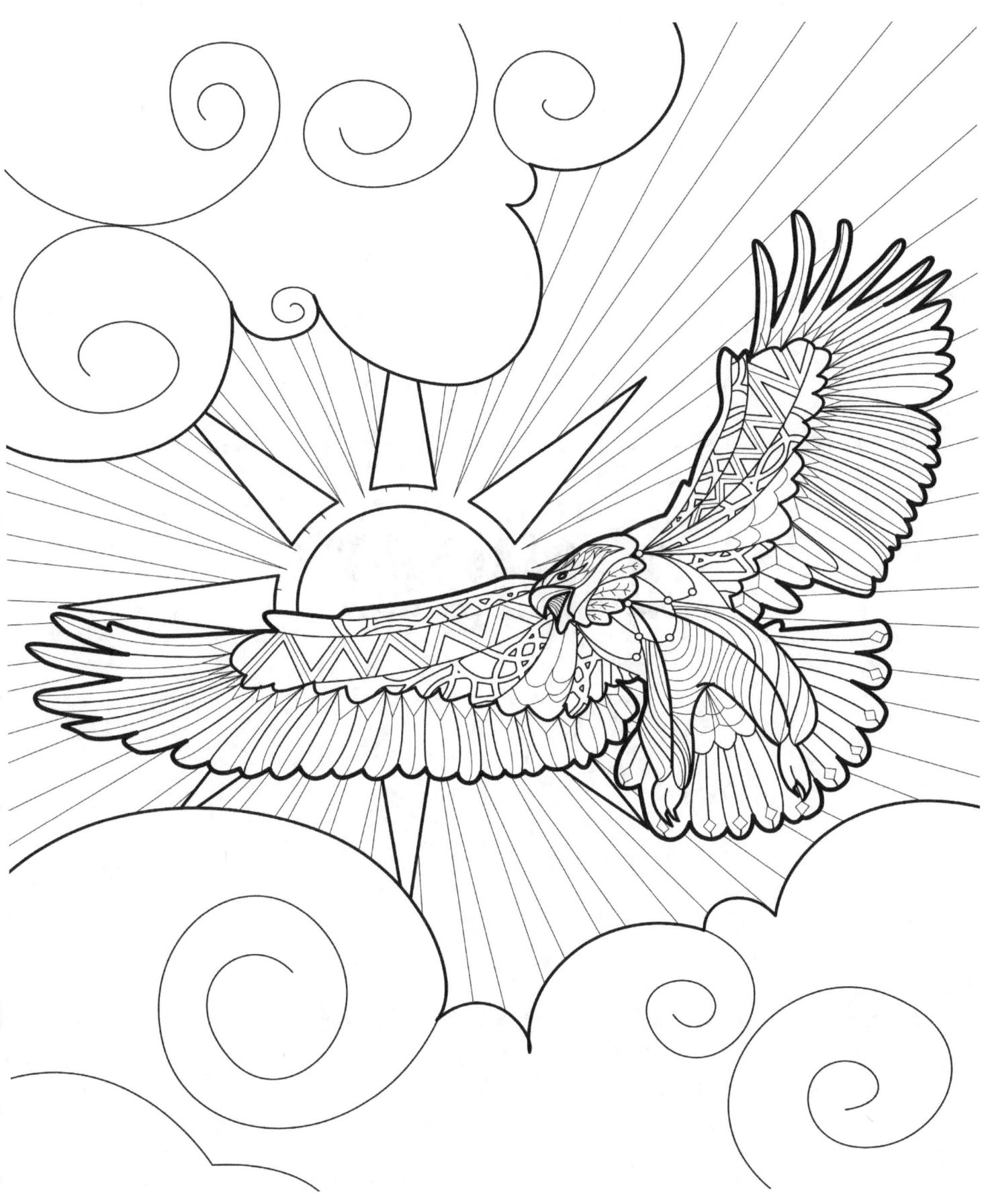

Badger

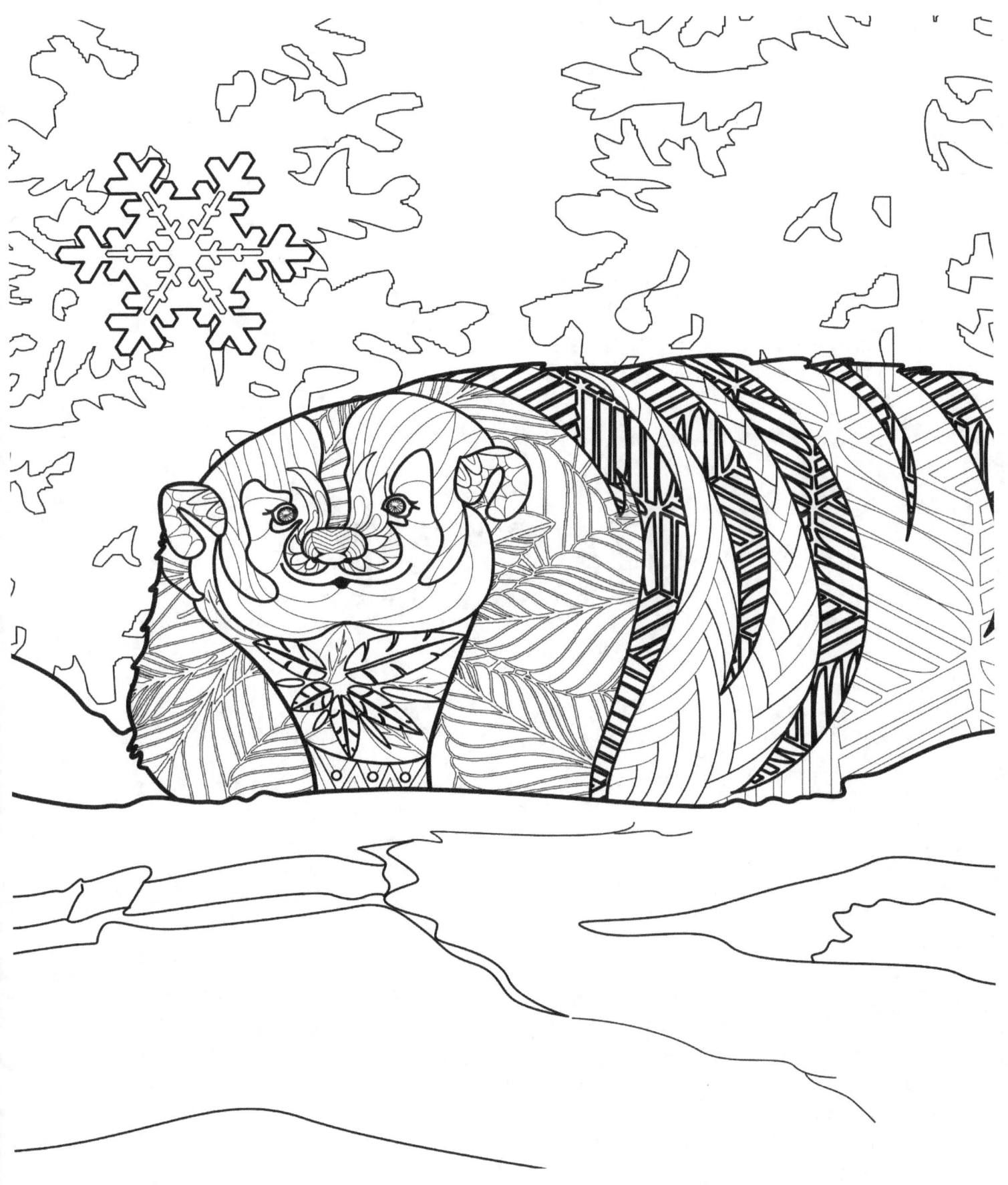

Beaver

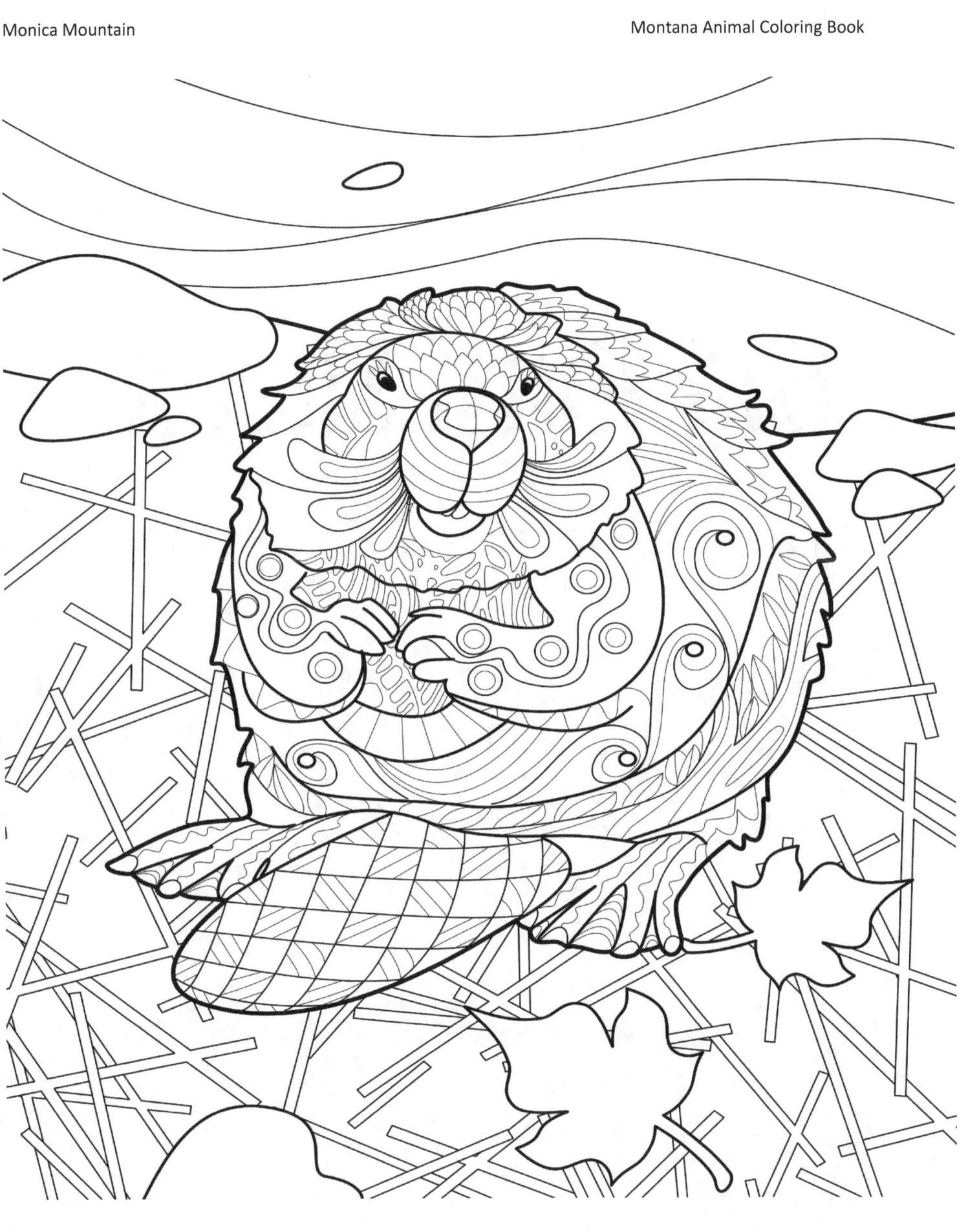

Big Horn Sheep

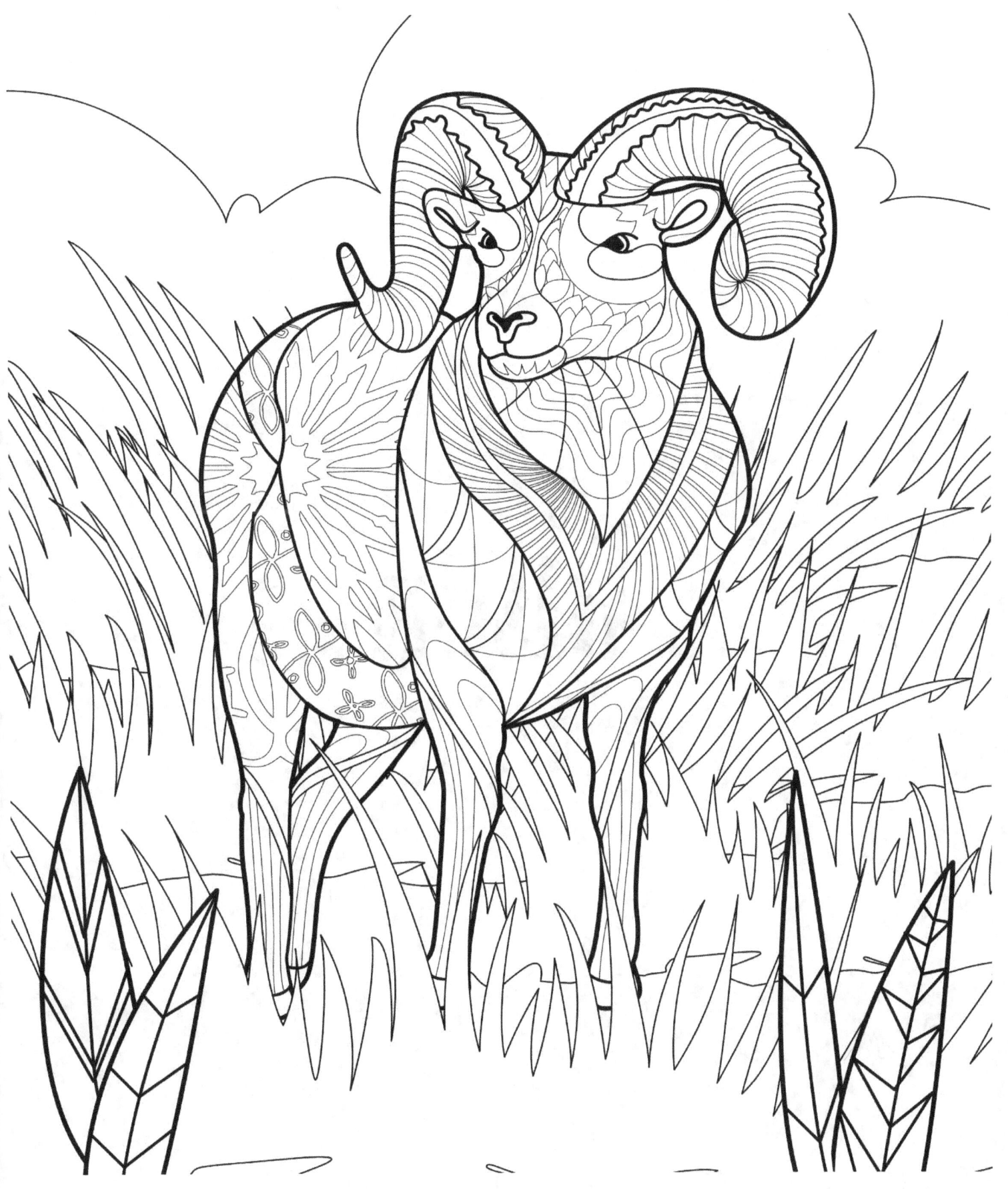

Bison

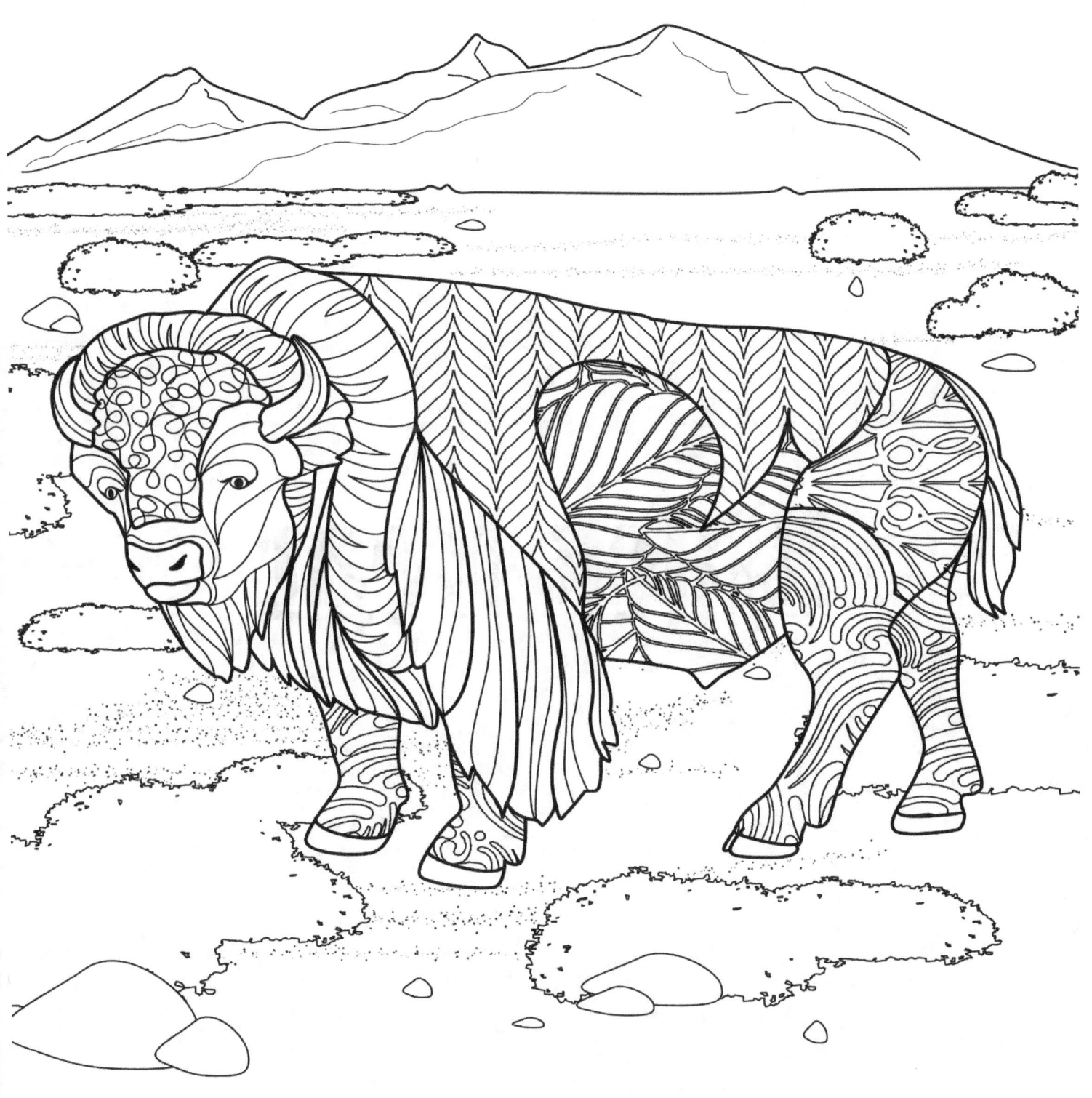

Black Bear

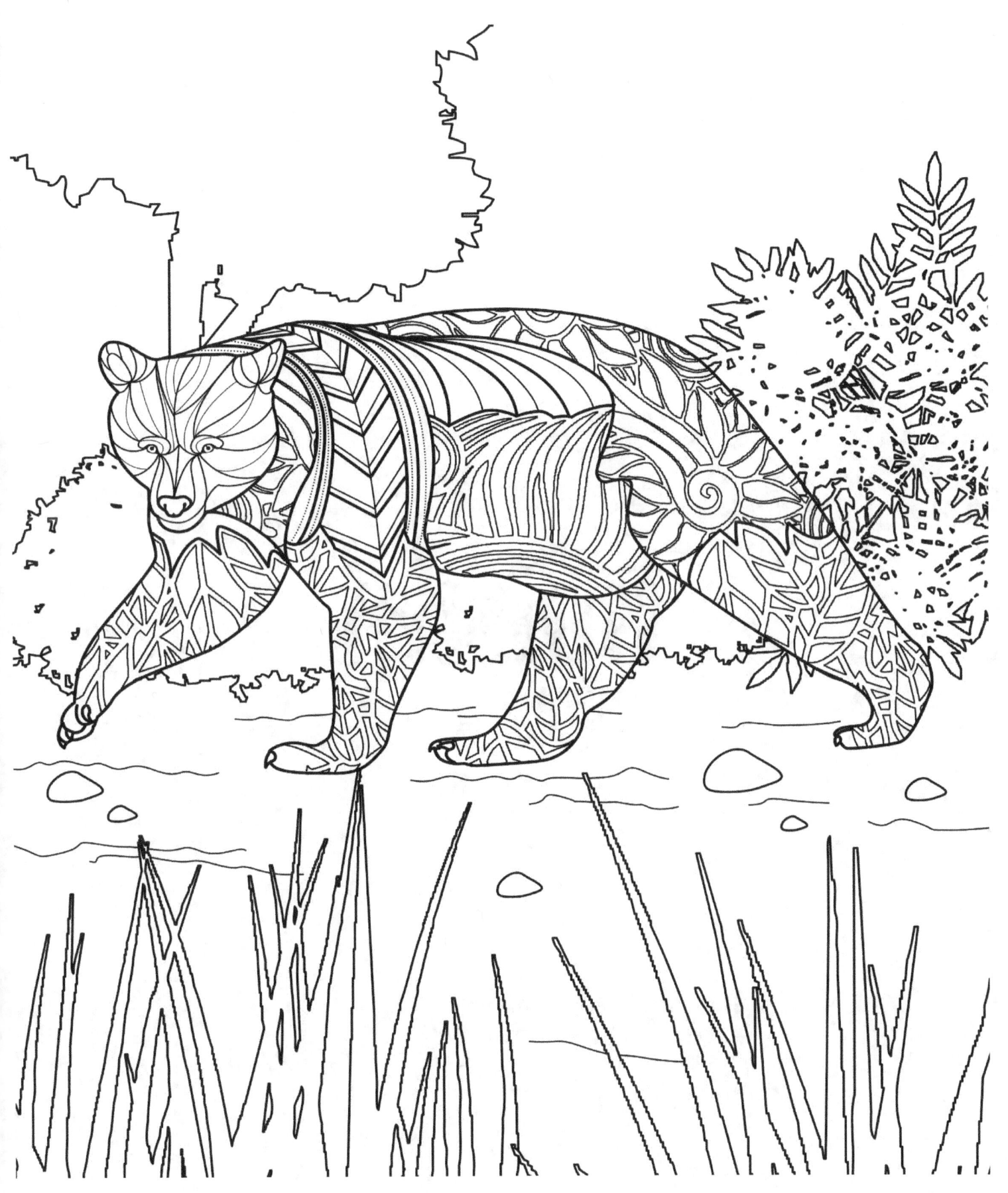

Bobcat

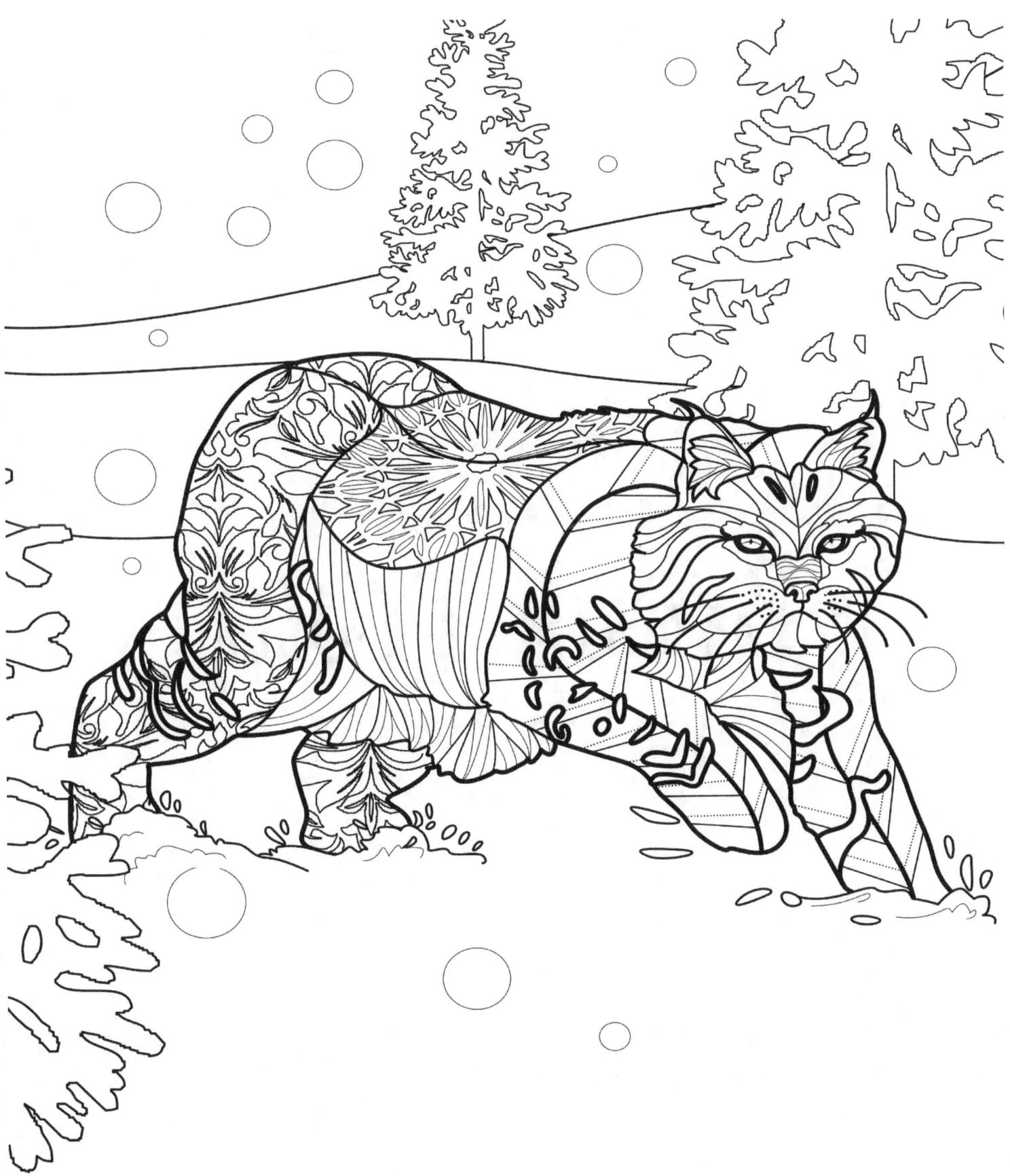

Brook Trout

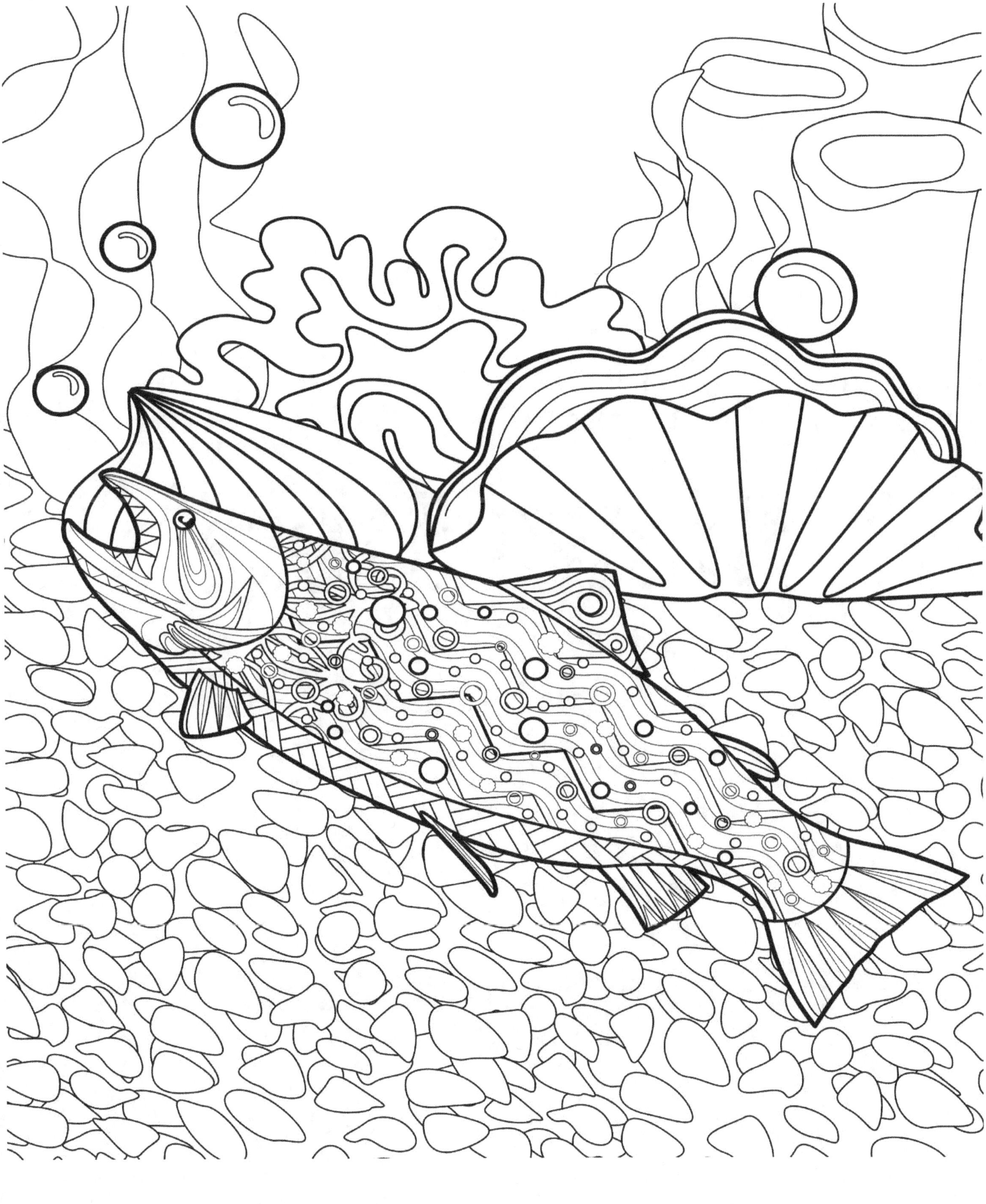

Brown Trout

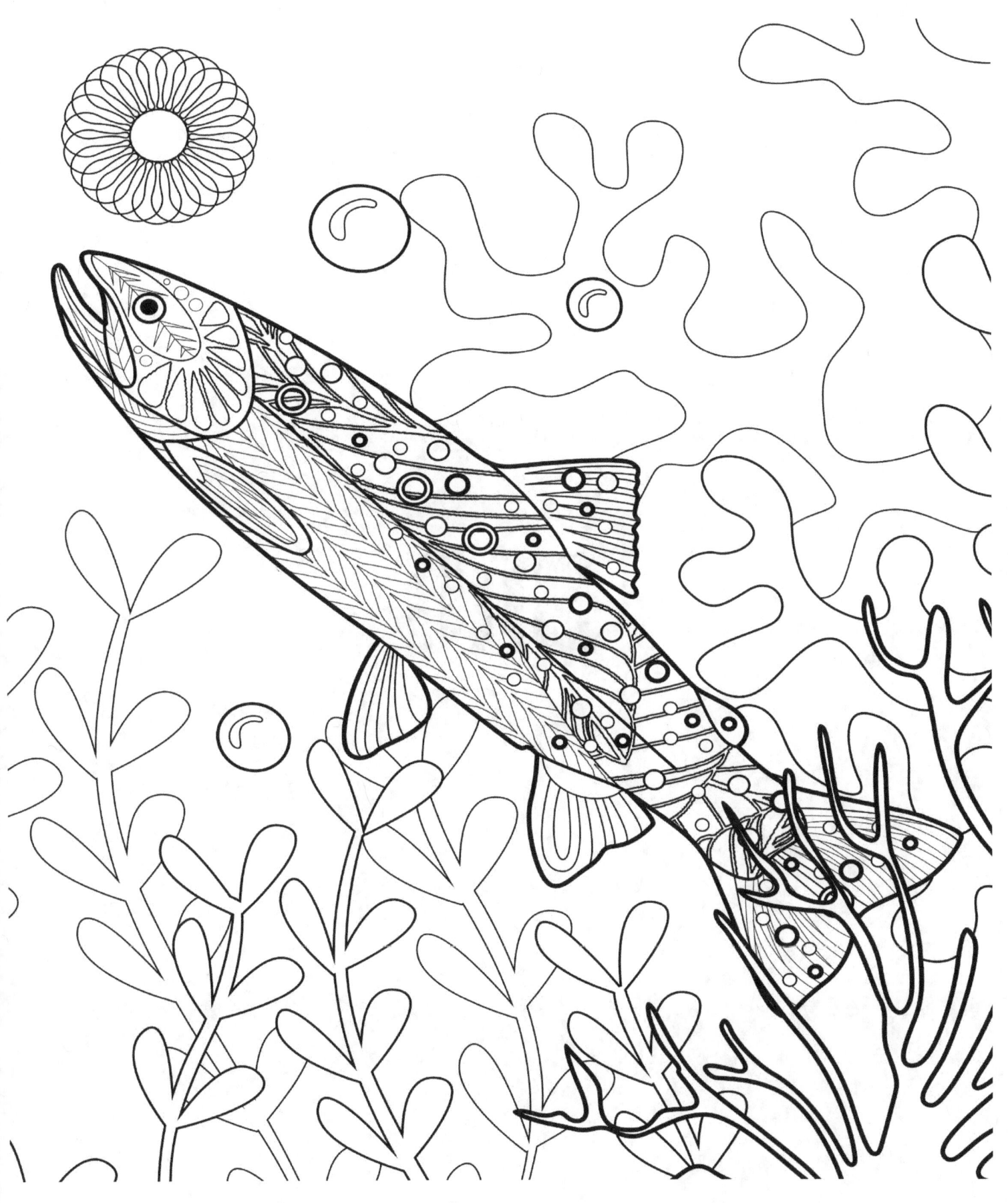

Bull

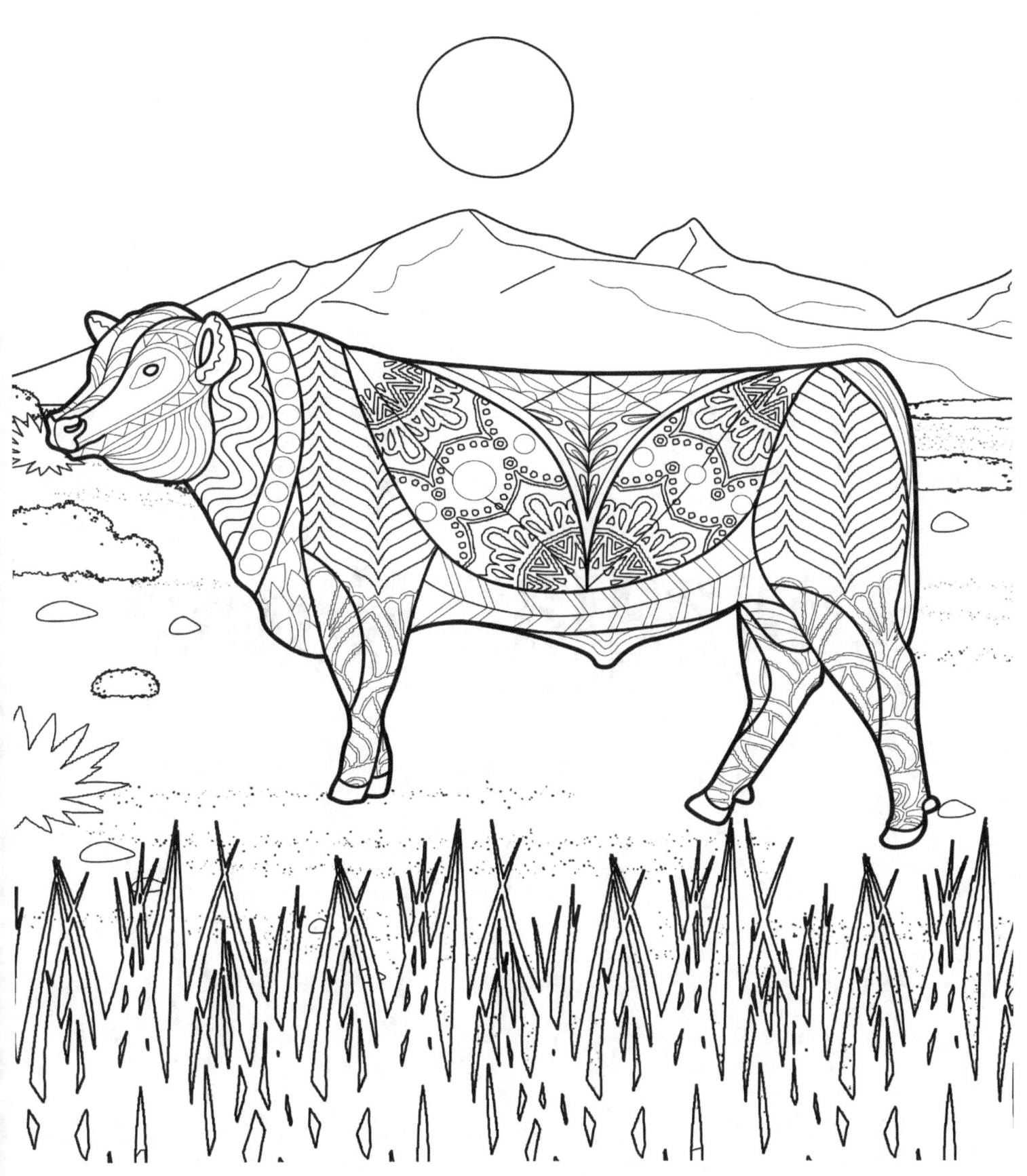

Canadian Goose

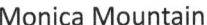

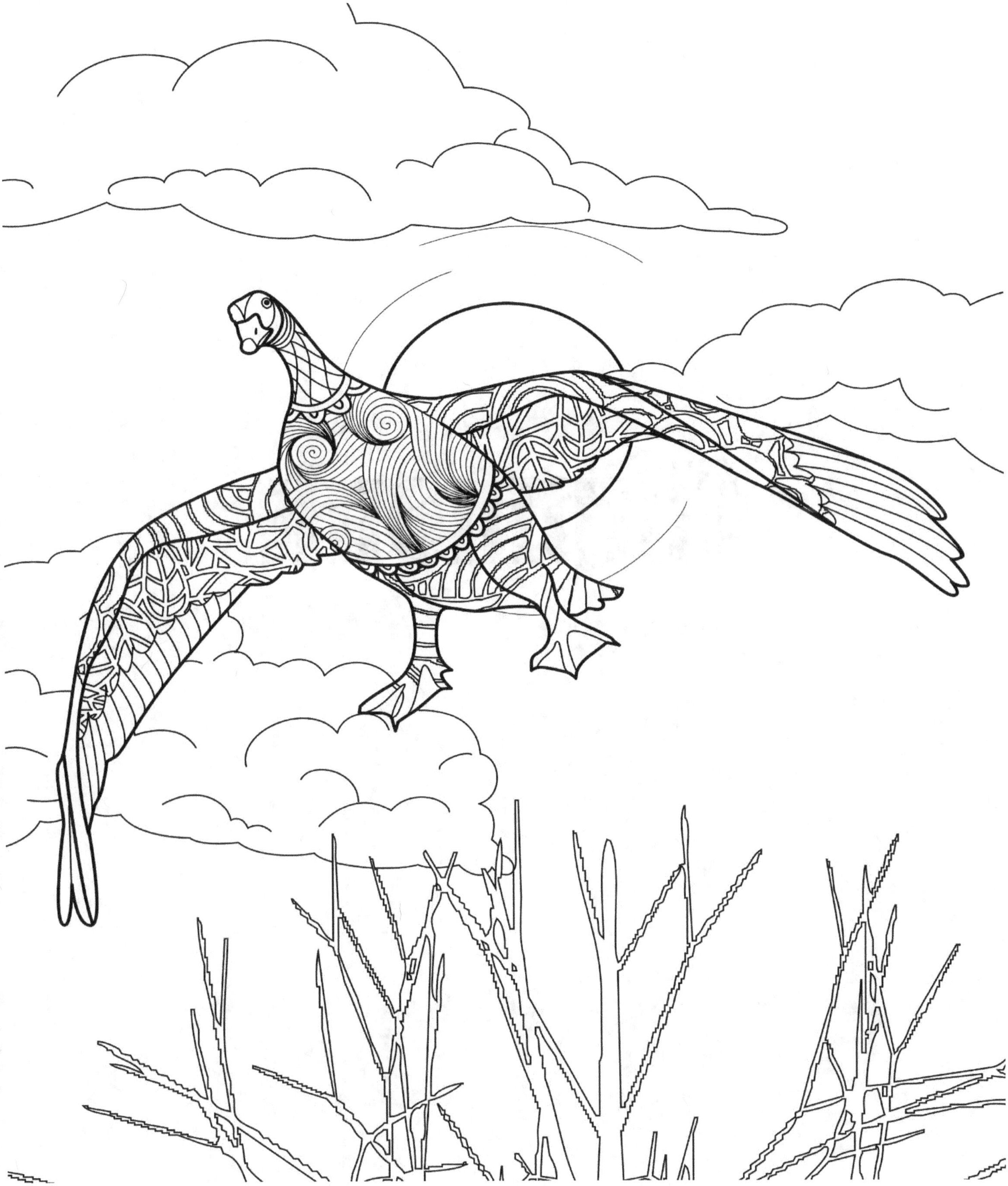

Chipmonk

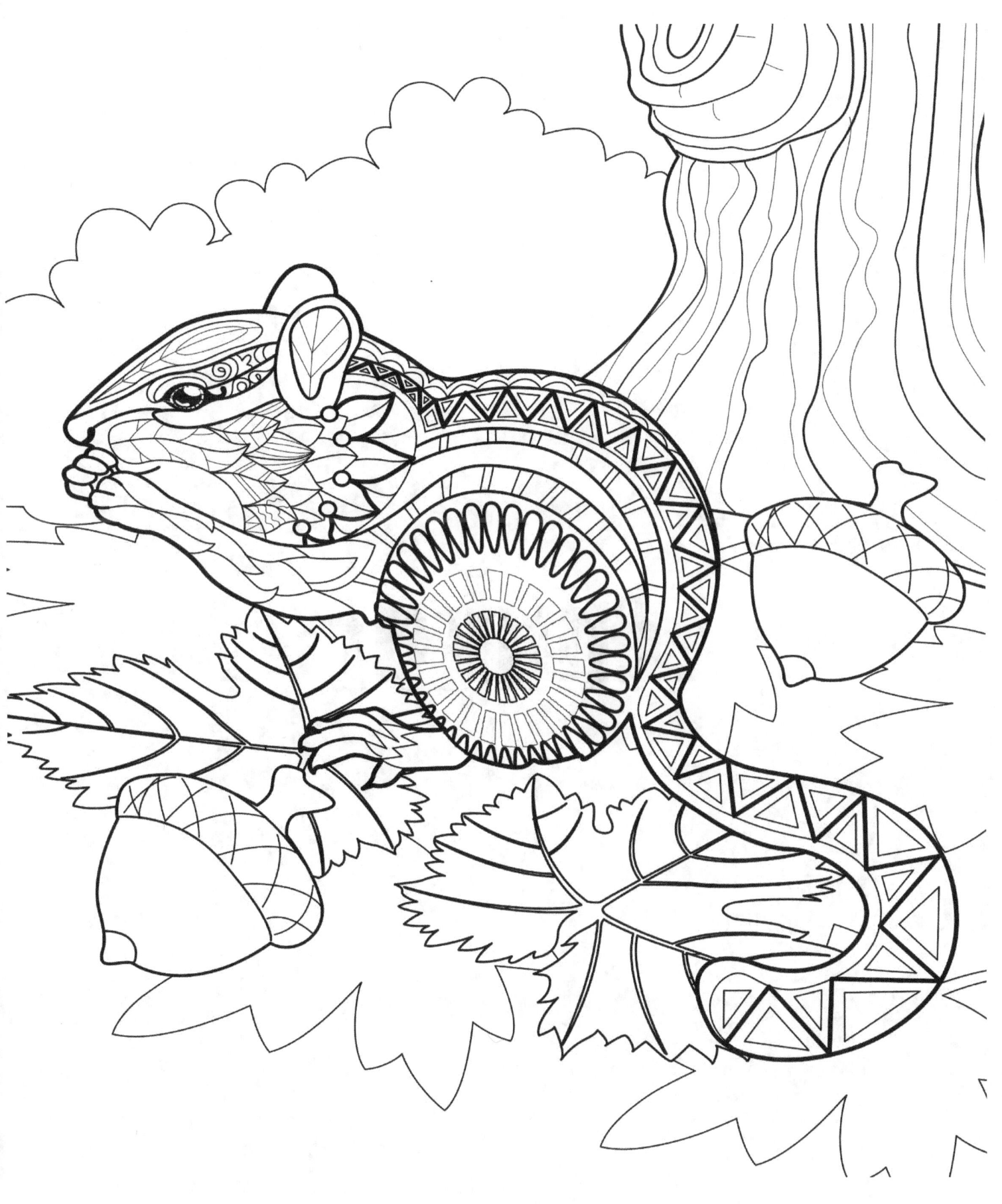

Chukar

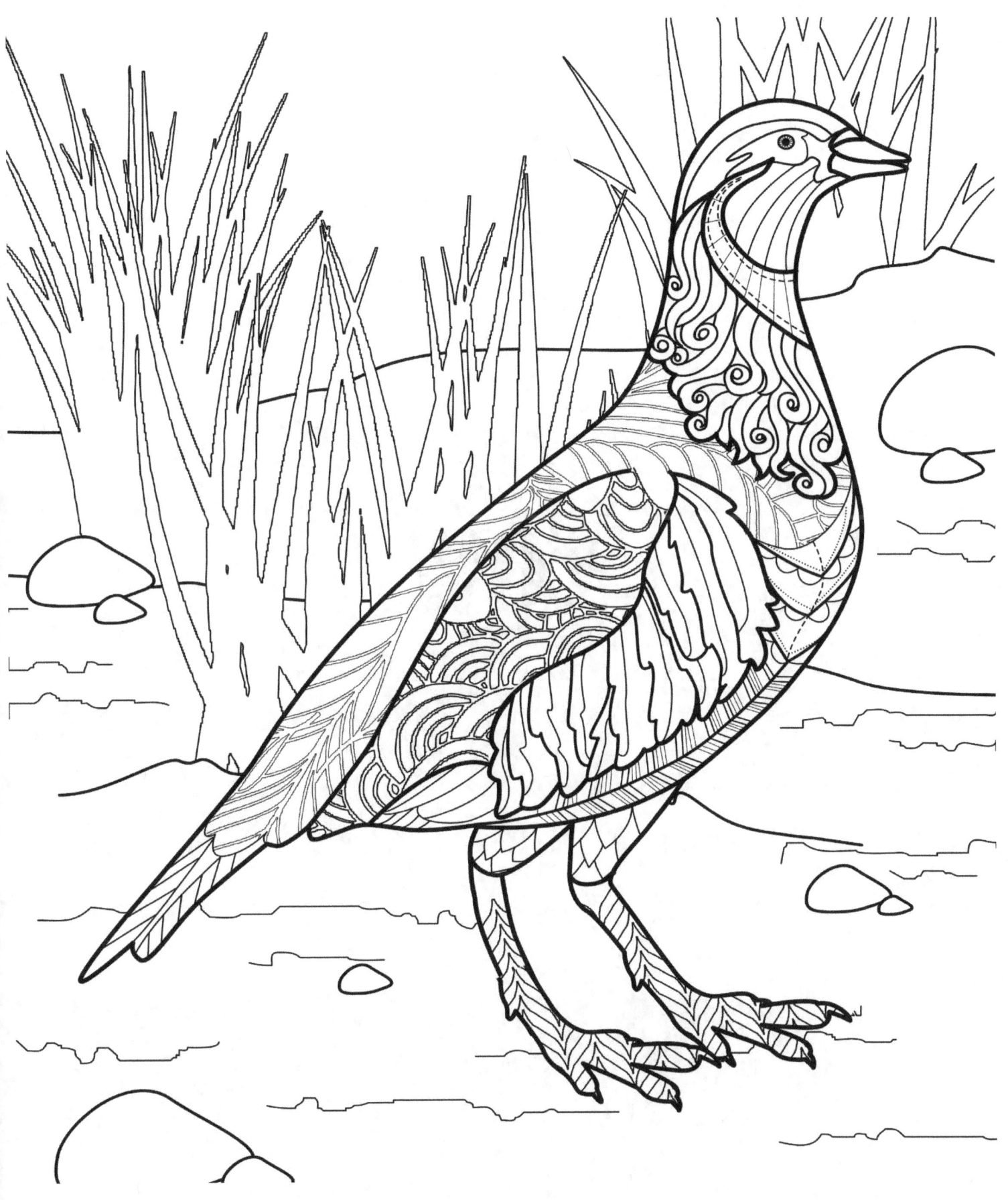

Cow

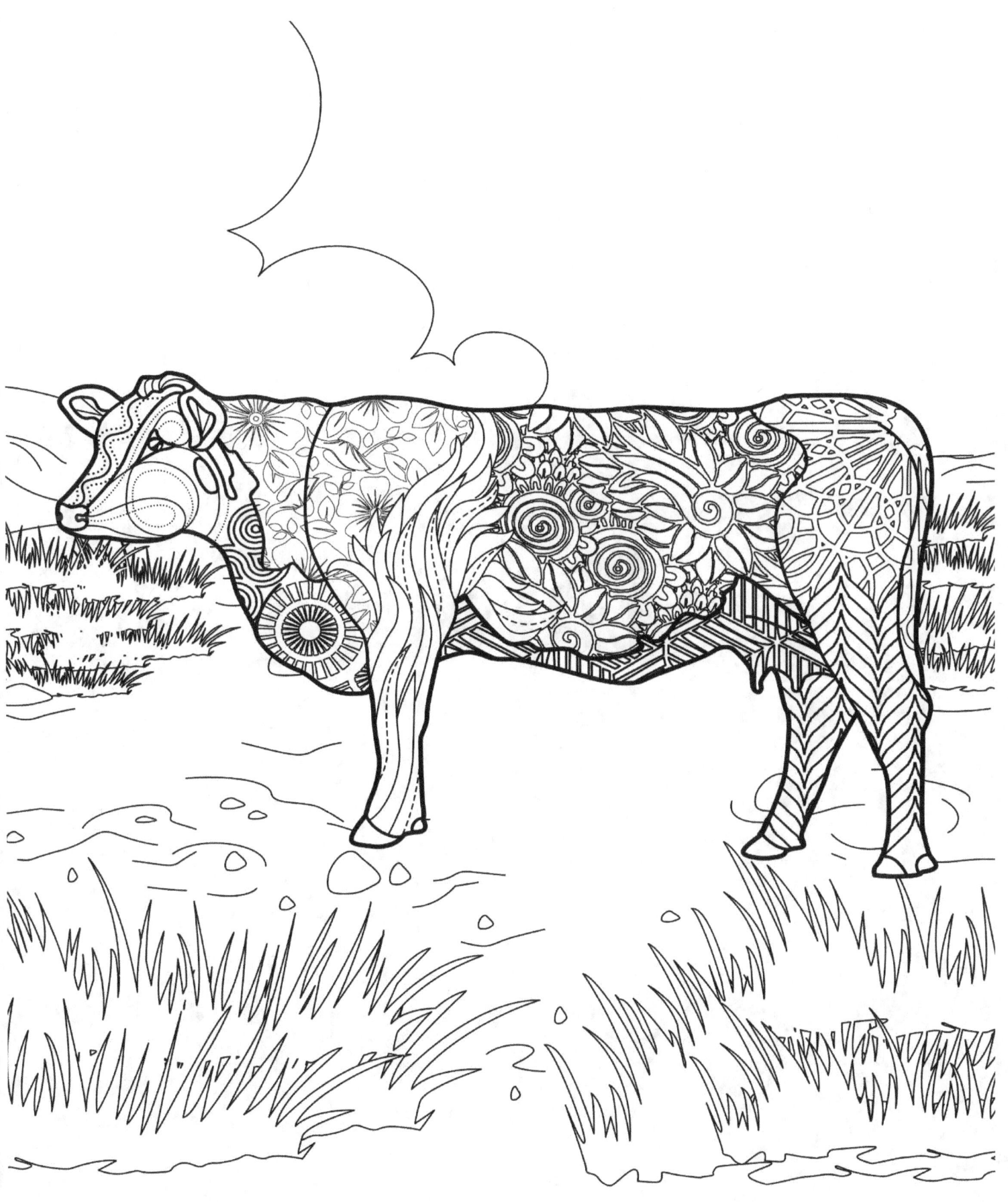

Coyote

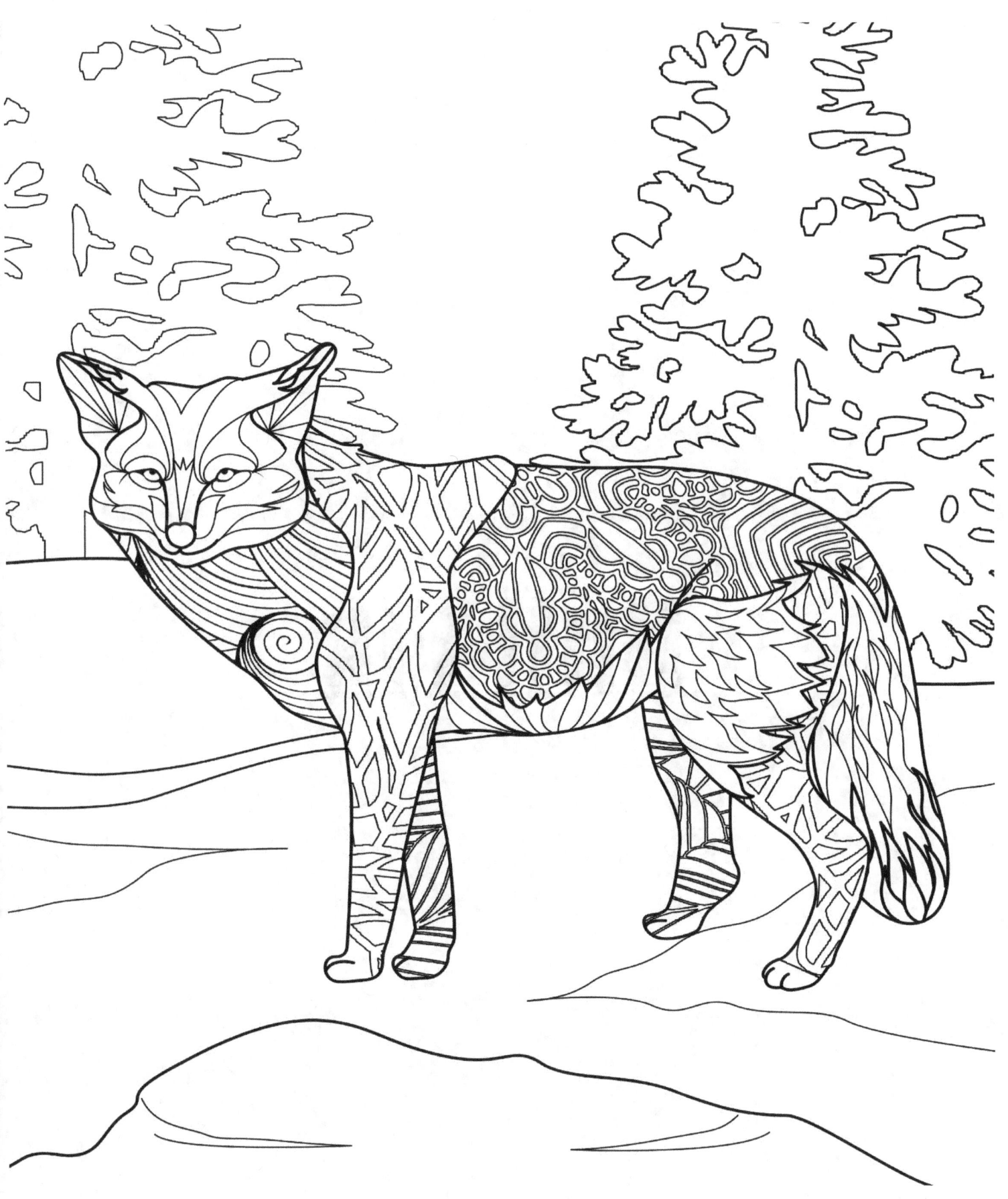

Bull Elk

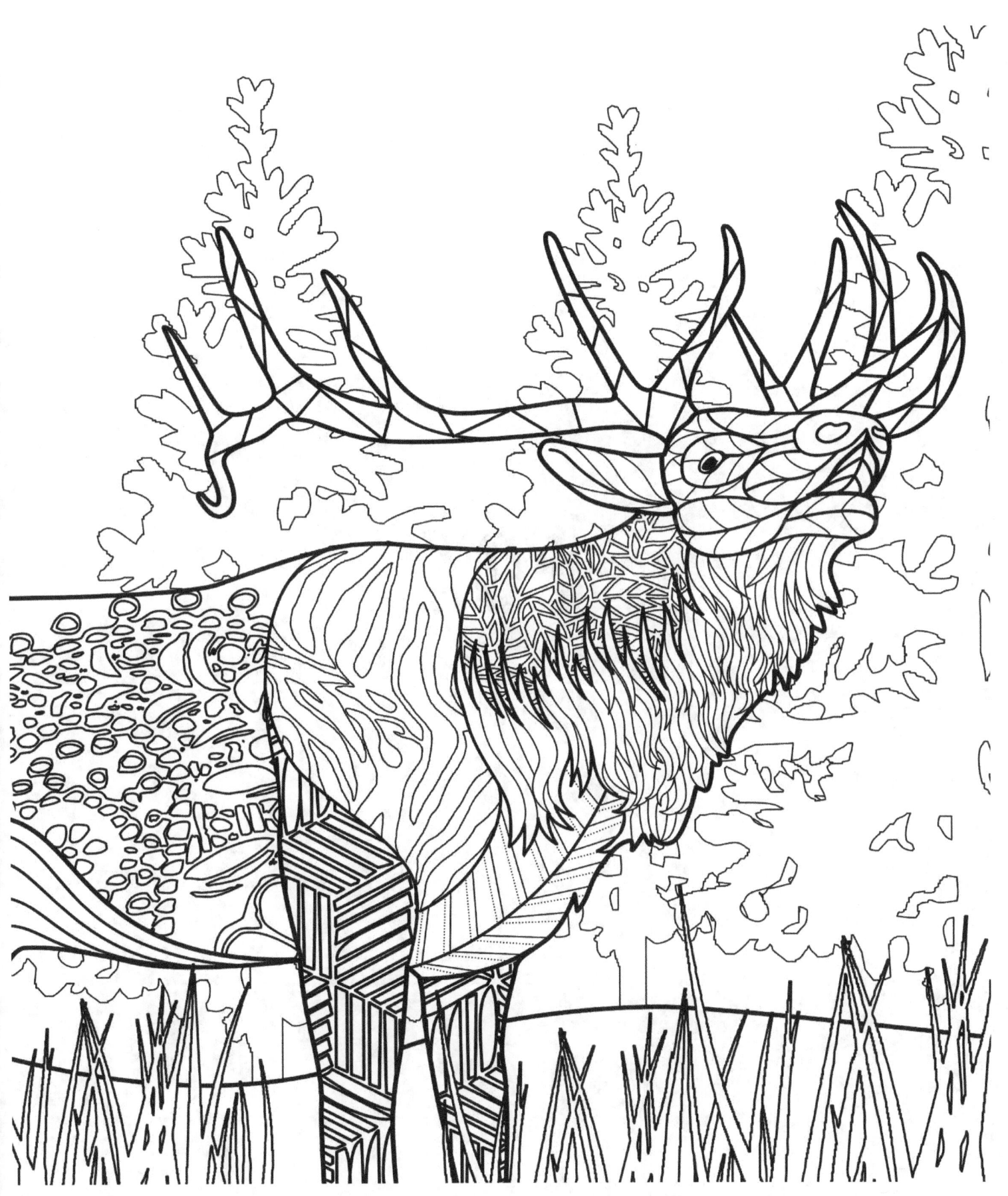

FOX

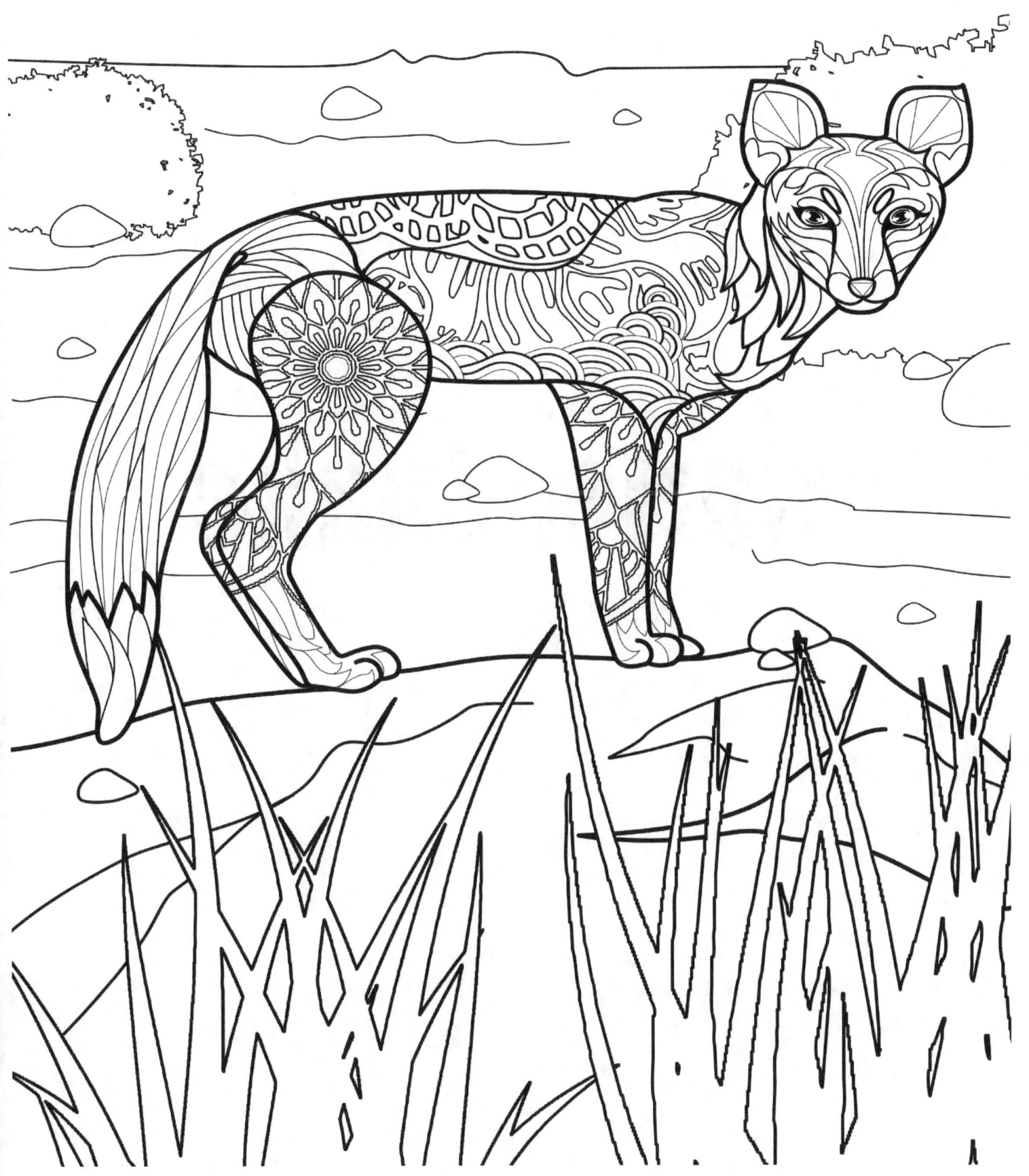

Garter Snake

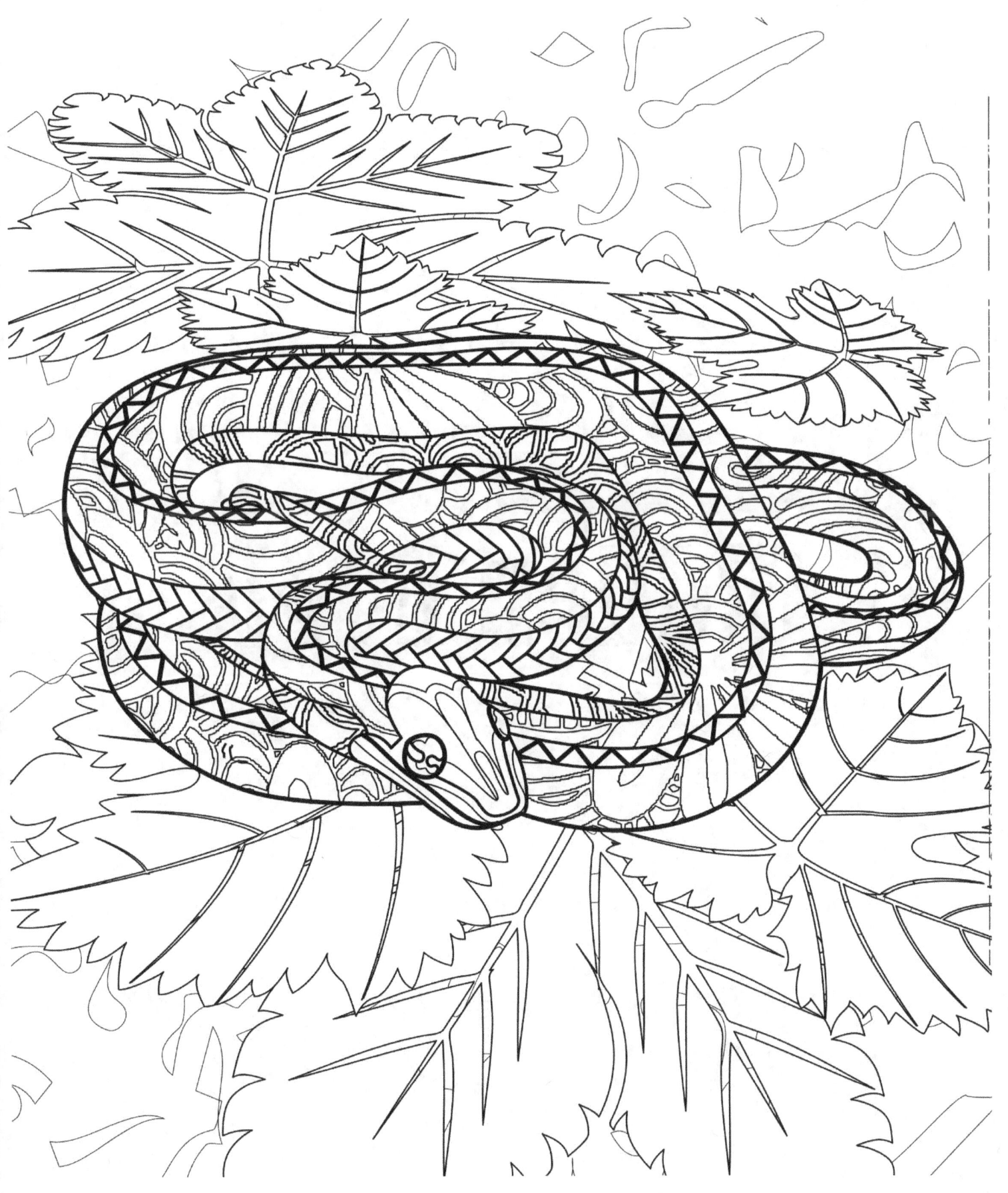

Golden Eagle

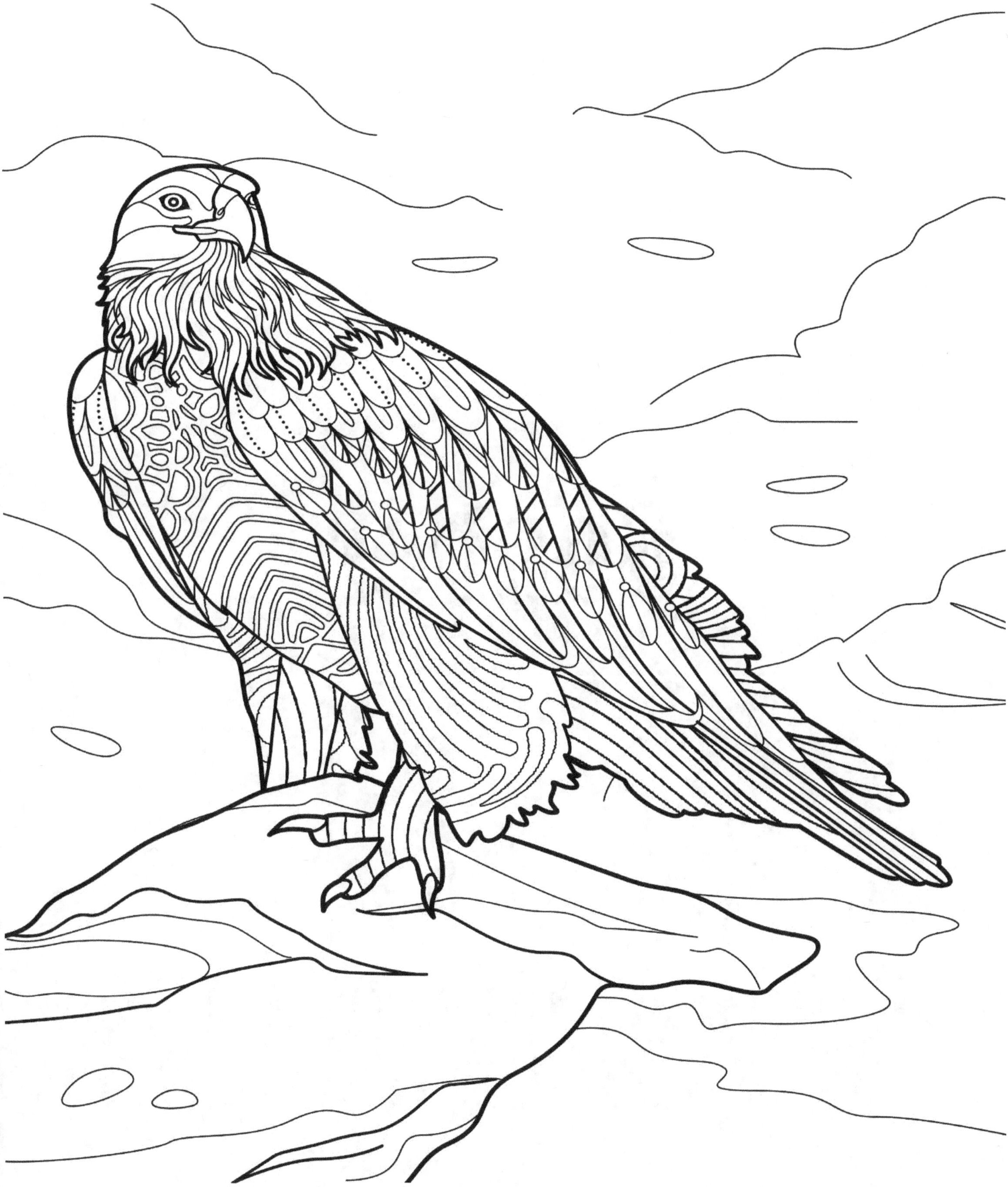

Gopher

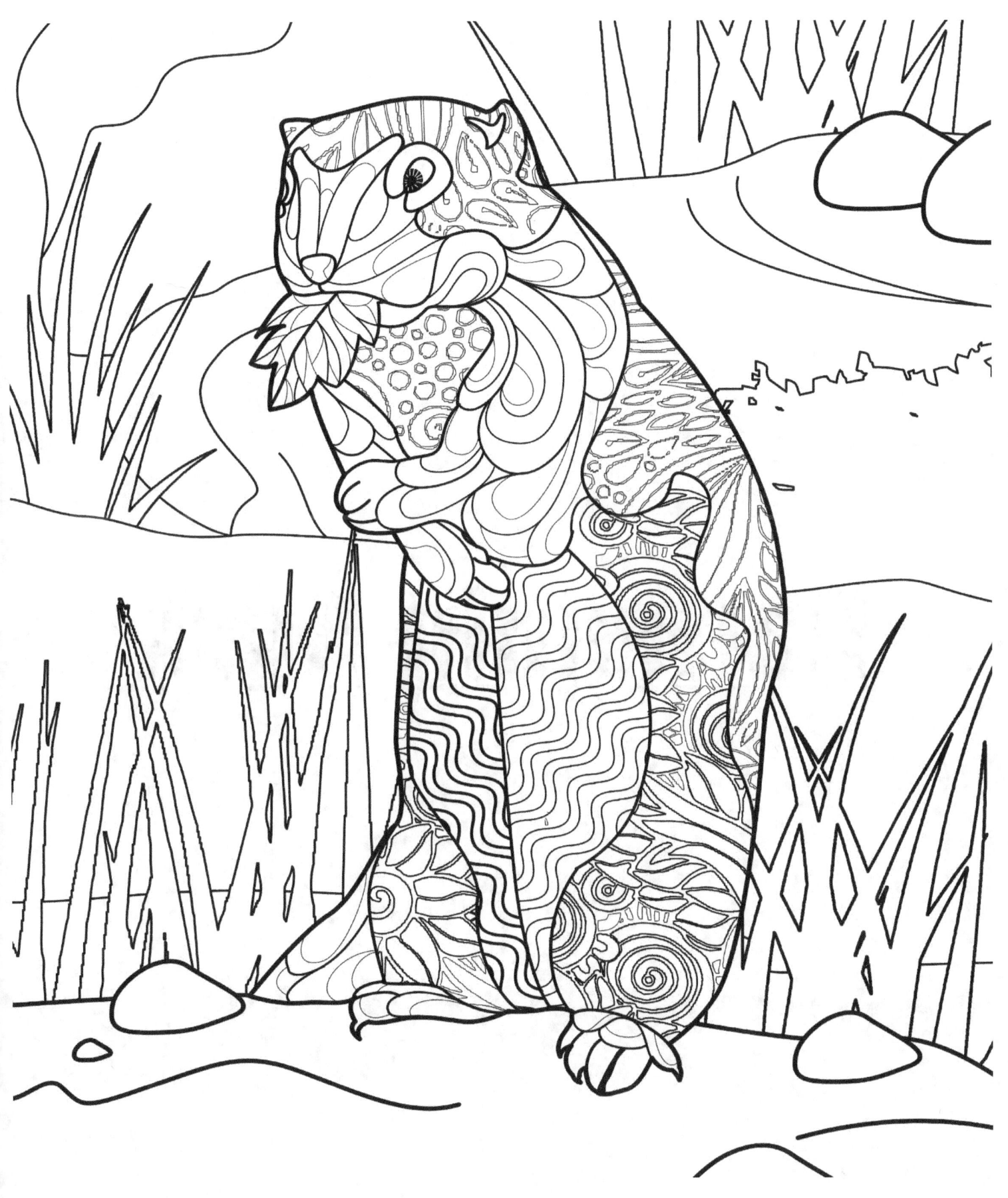

Harlequin Duck

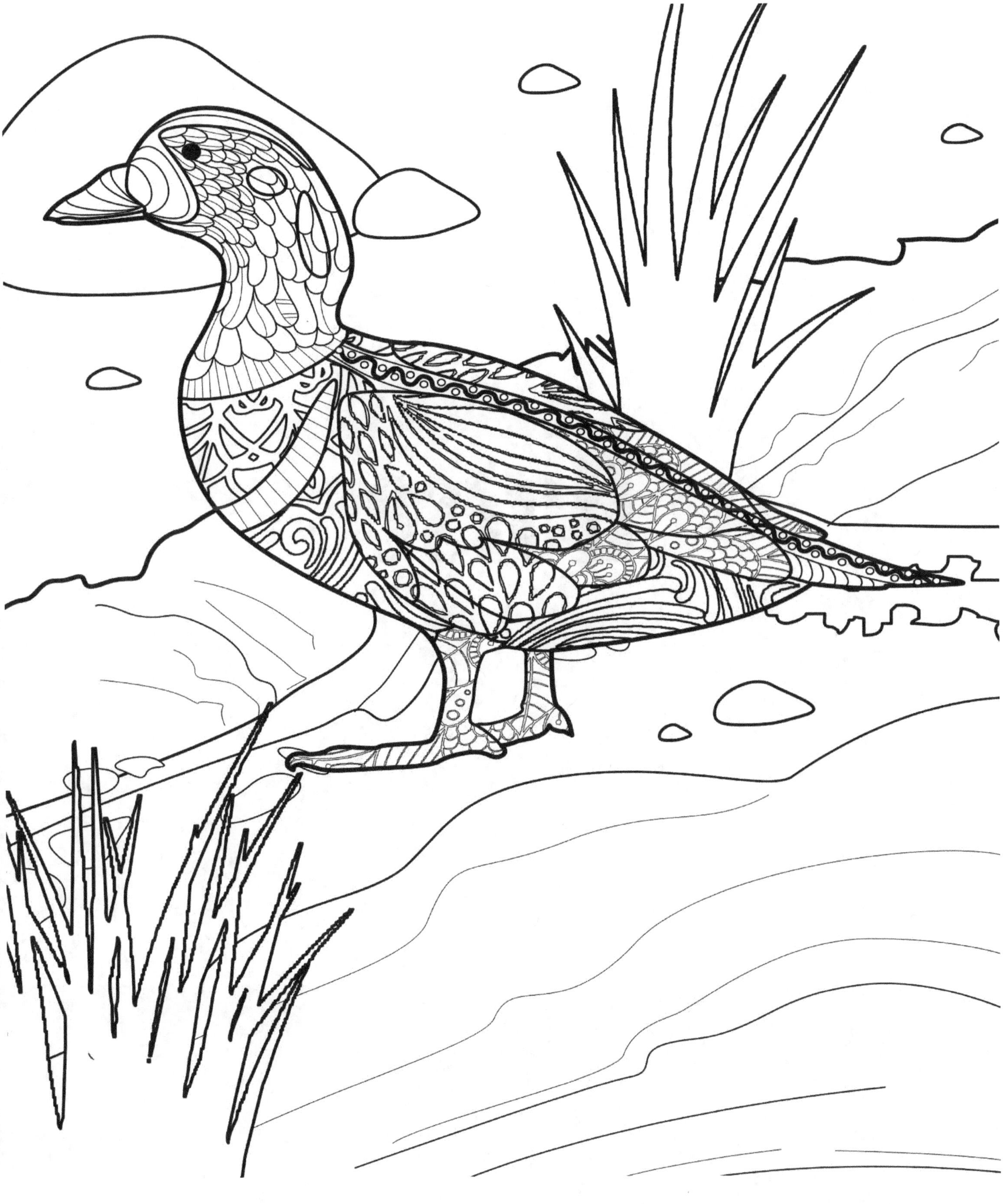

Horse

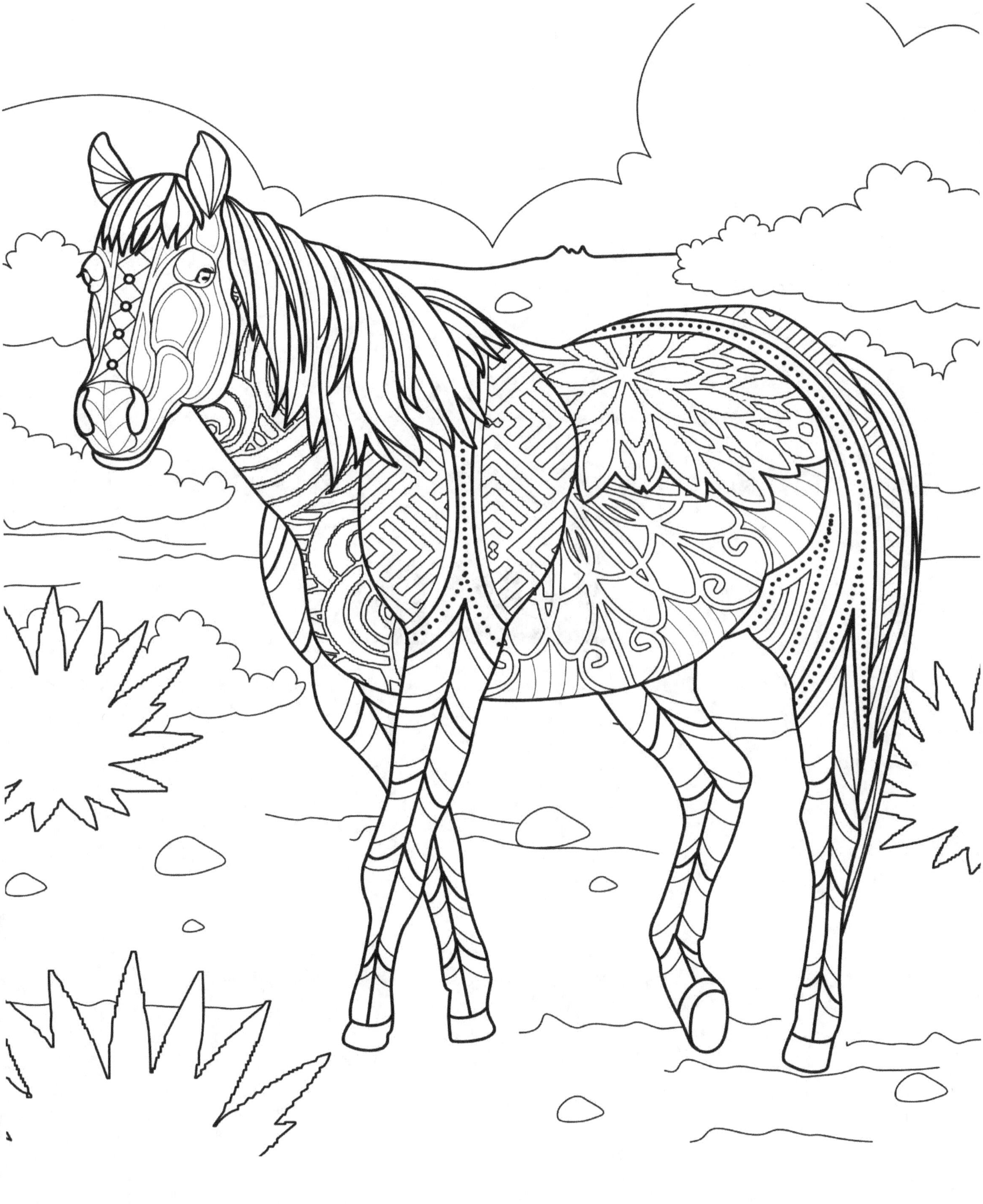

Loon

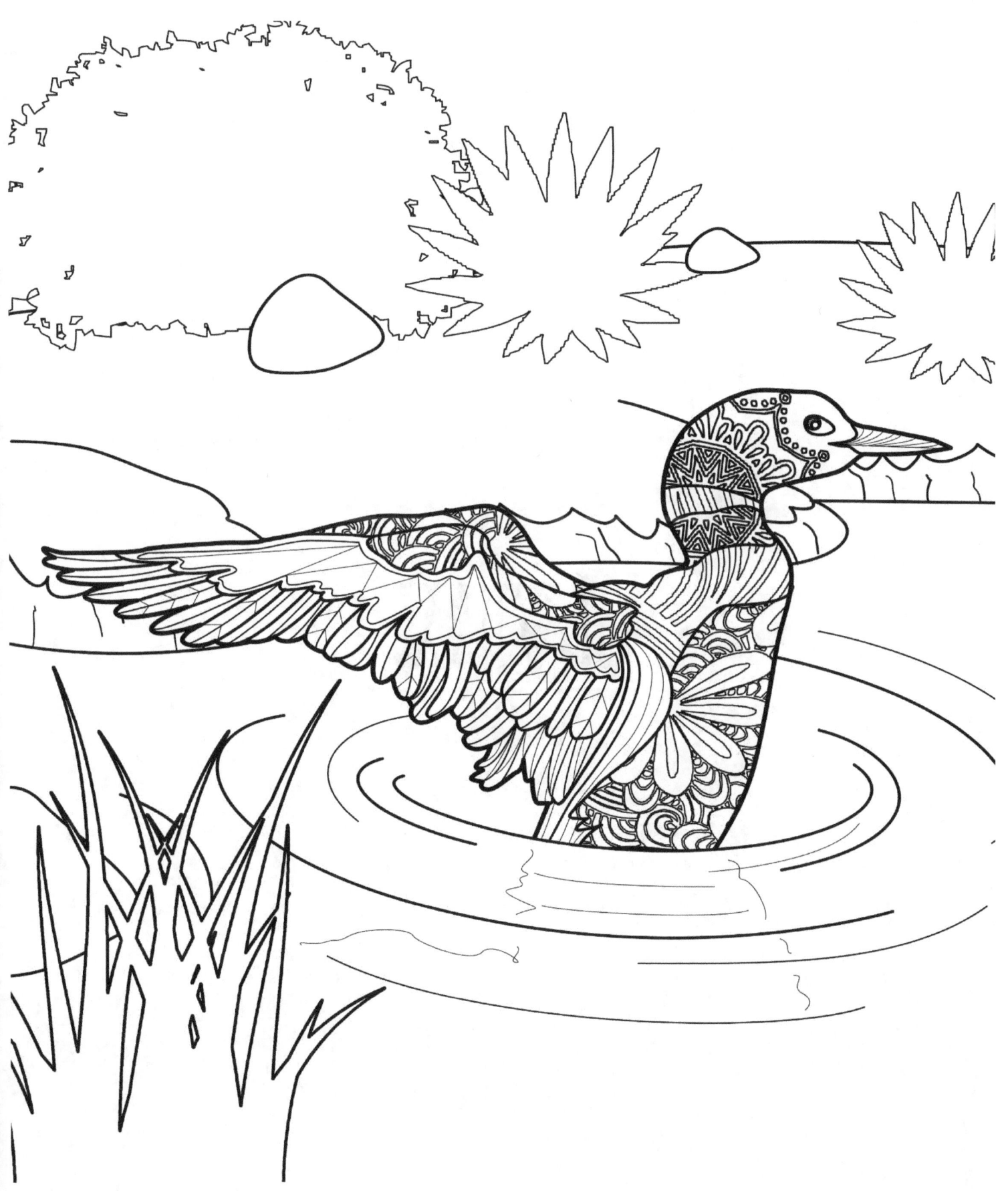

Lynx

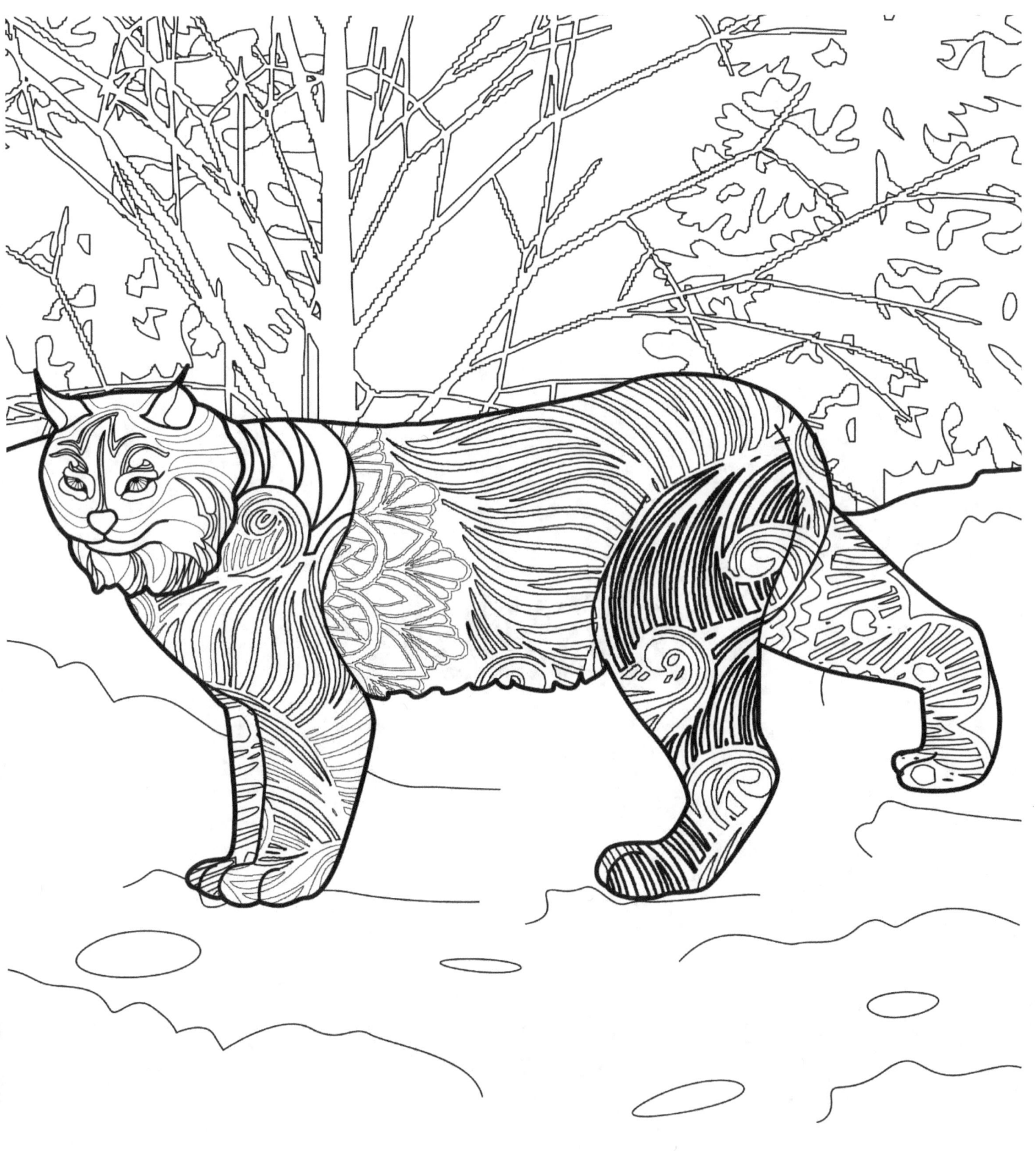

Magpie

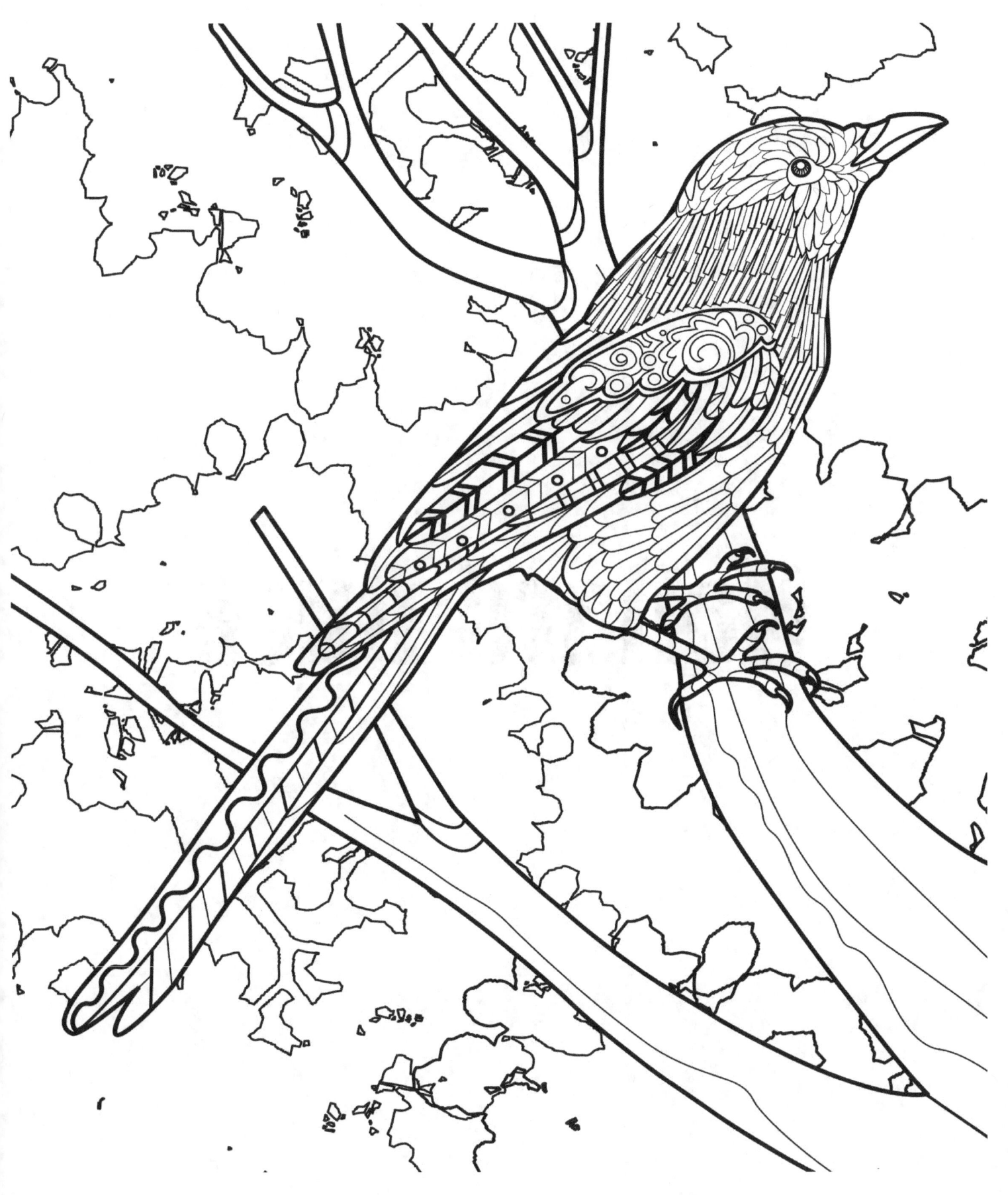

Mallard Duck

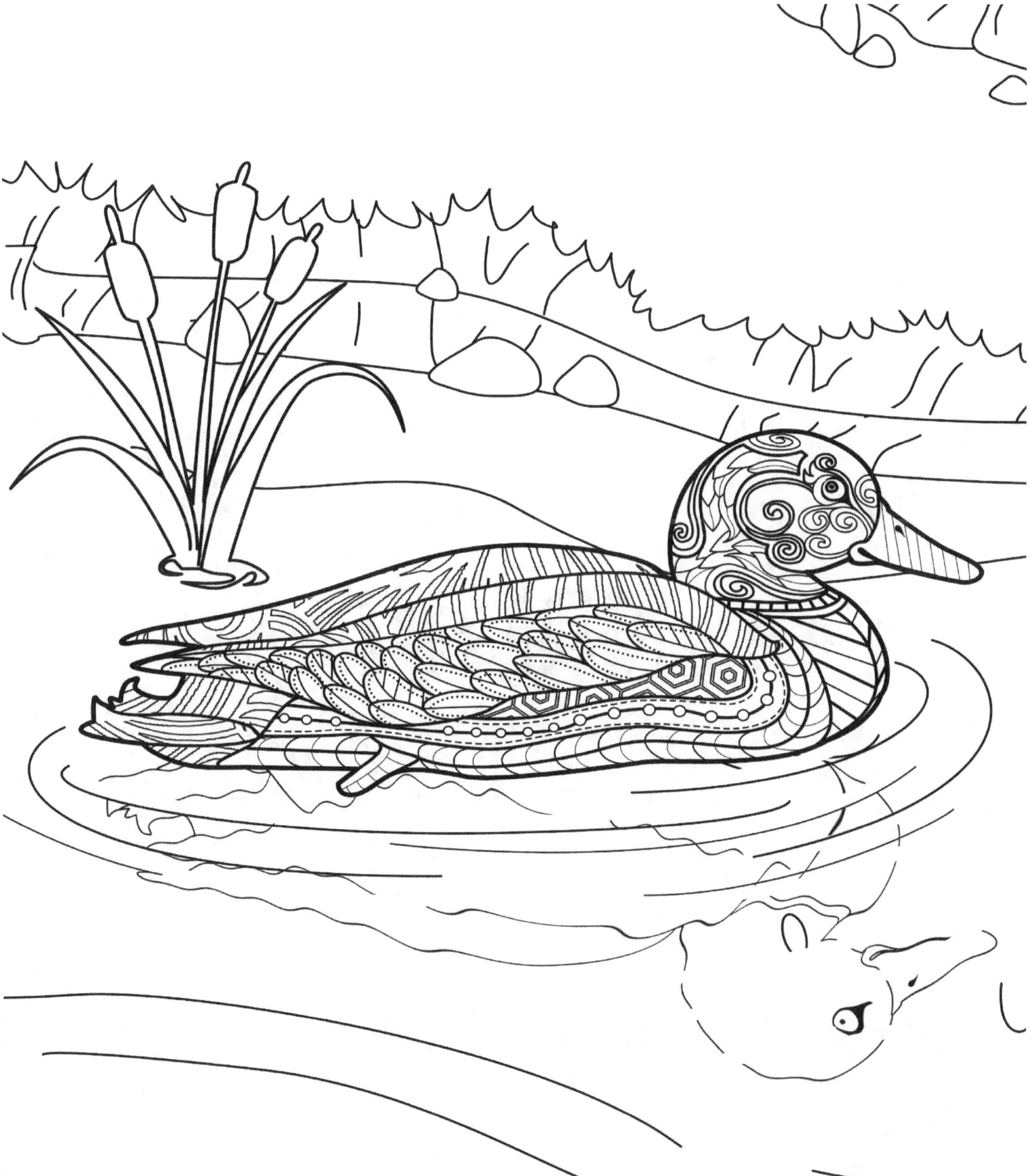

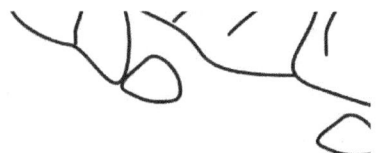

Martin

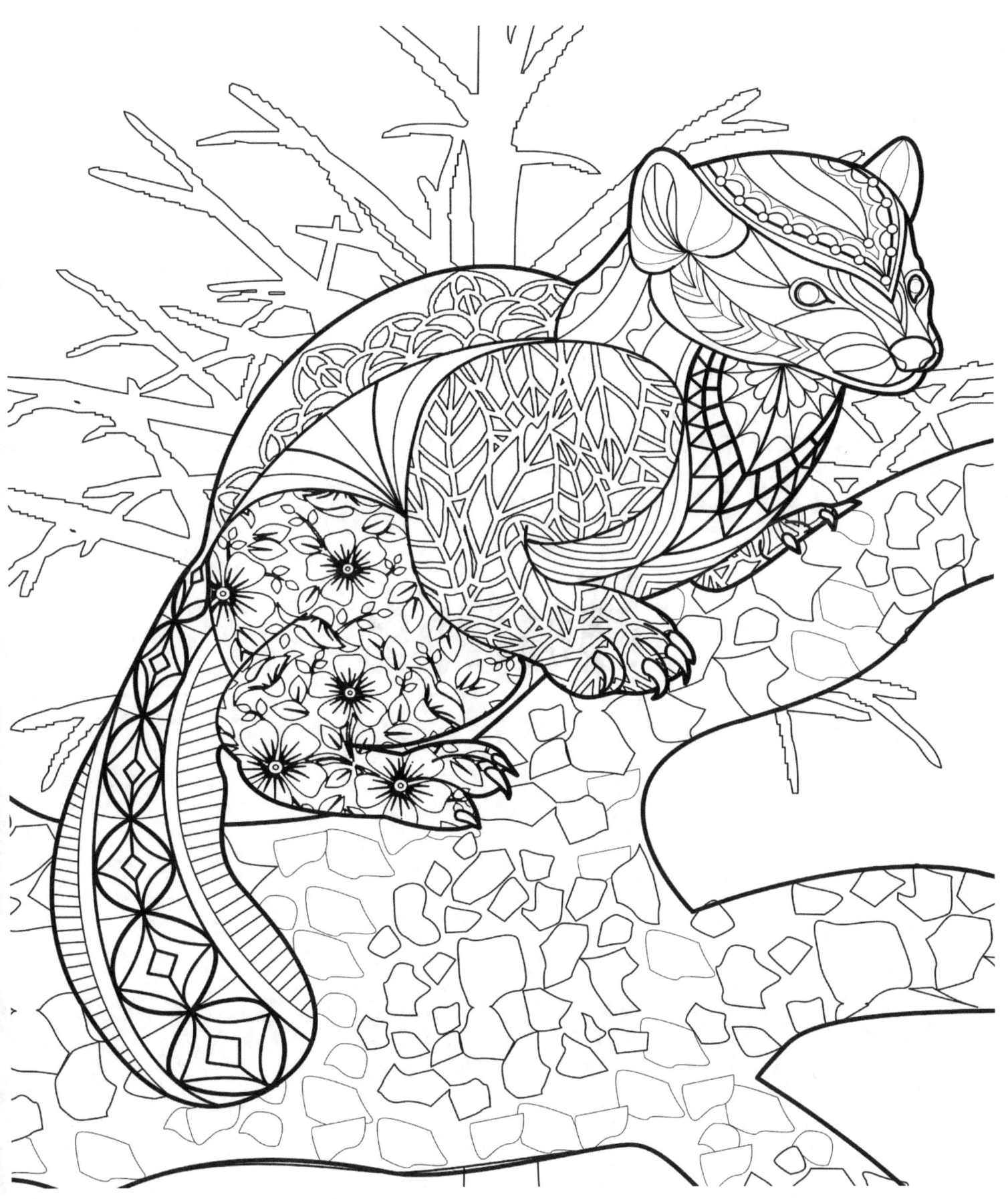

Moose

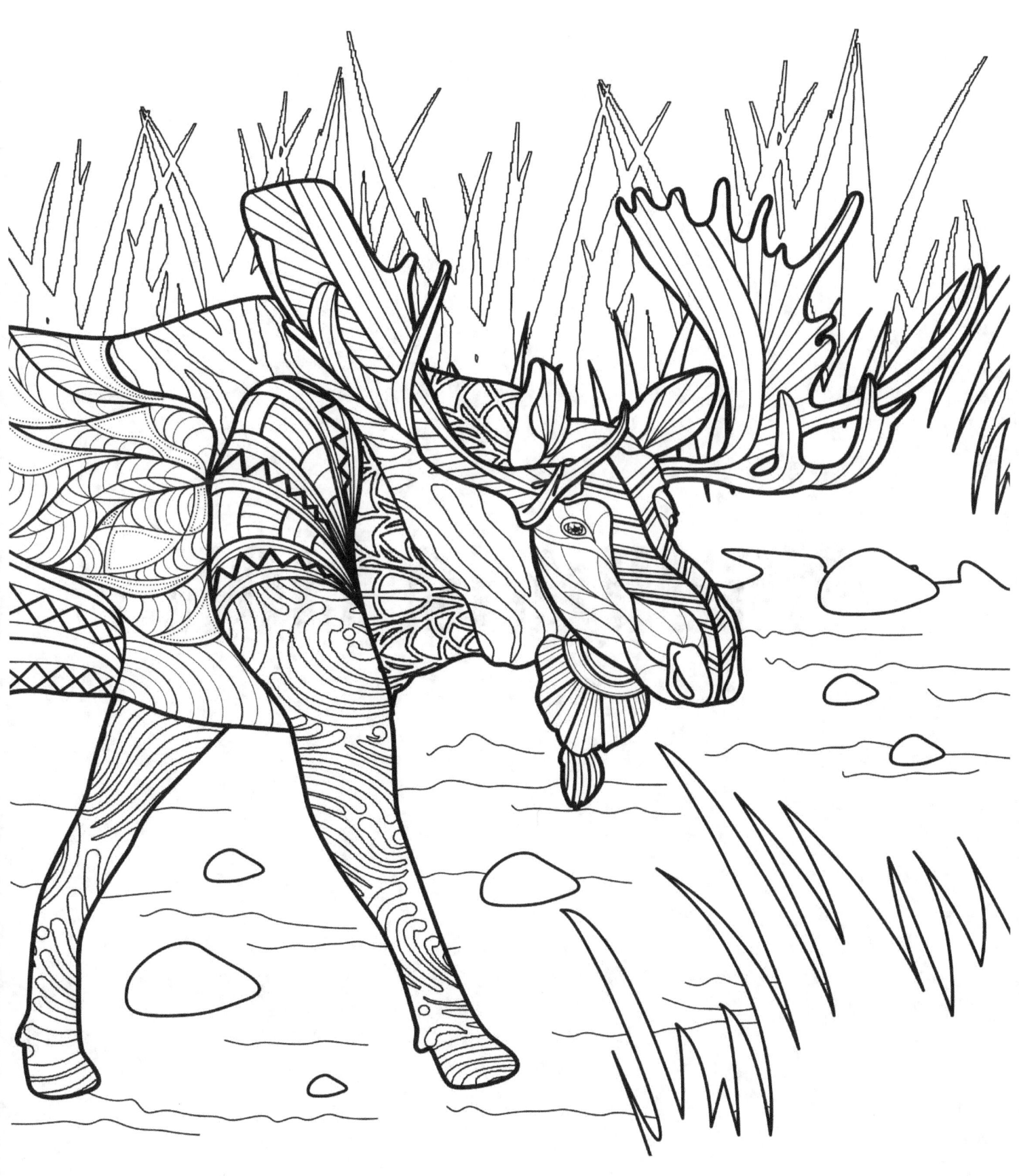

Mountain Lion

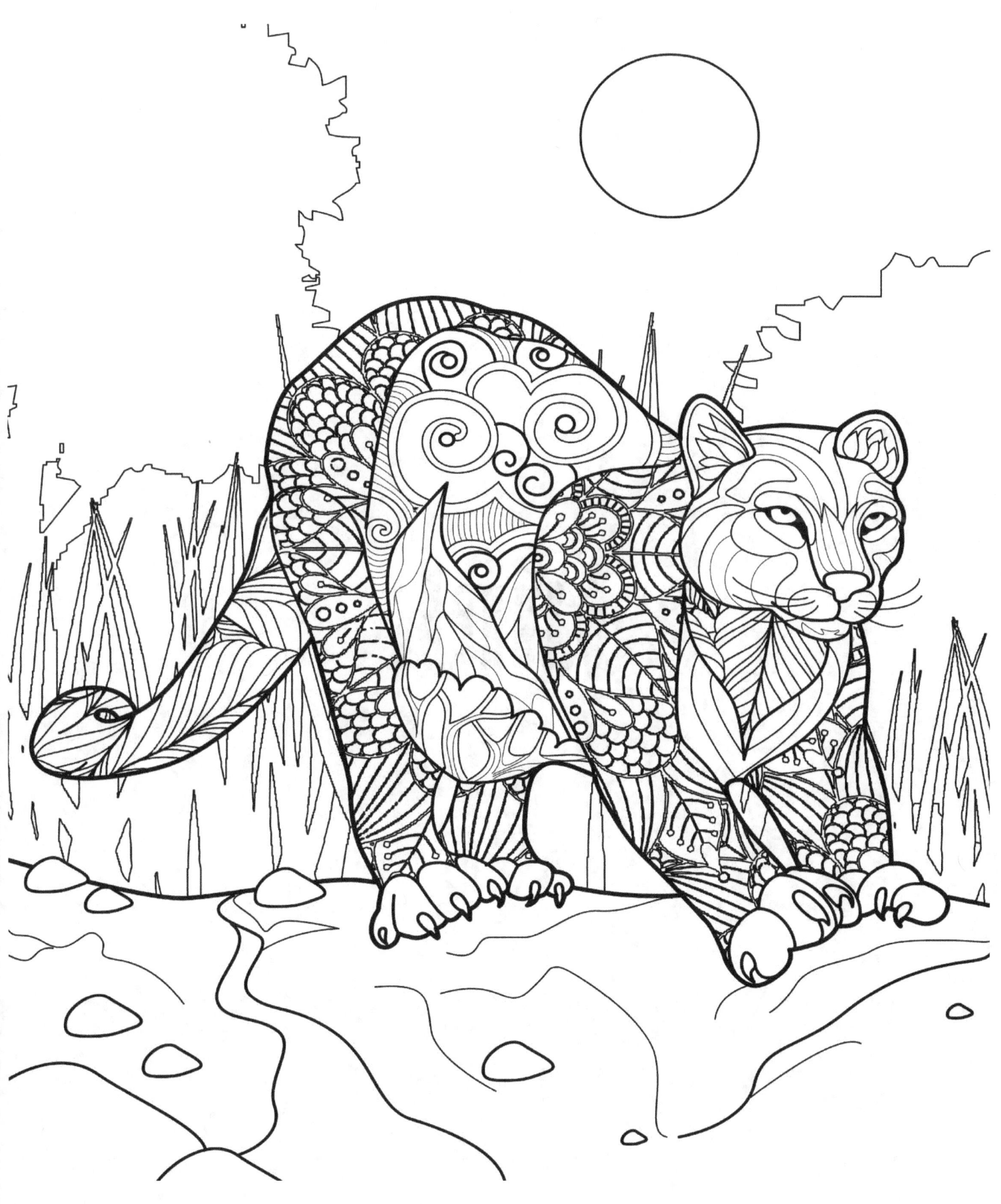

Mink

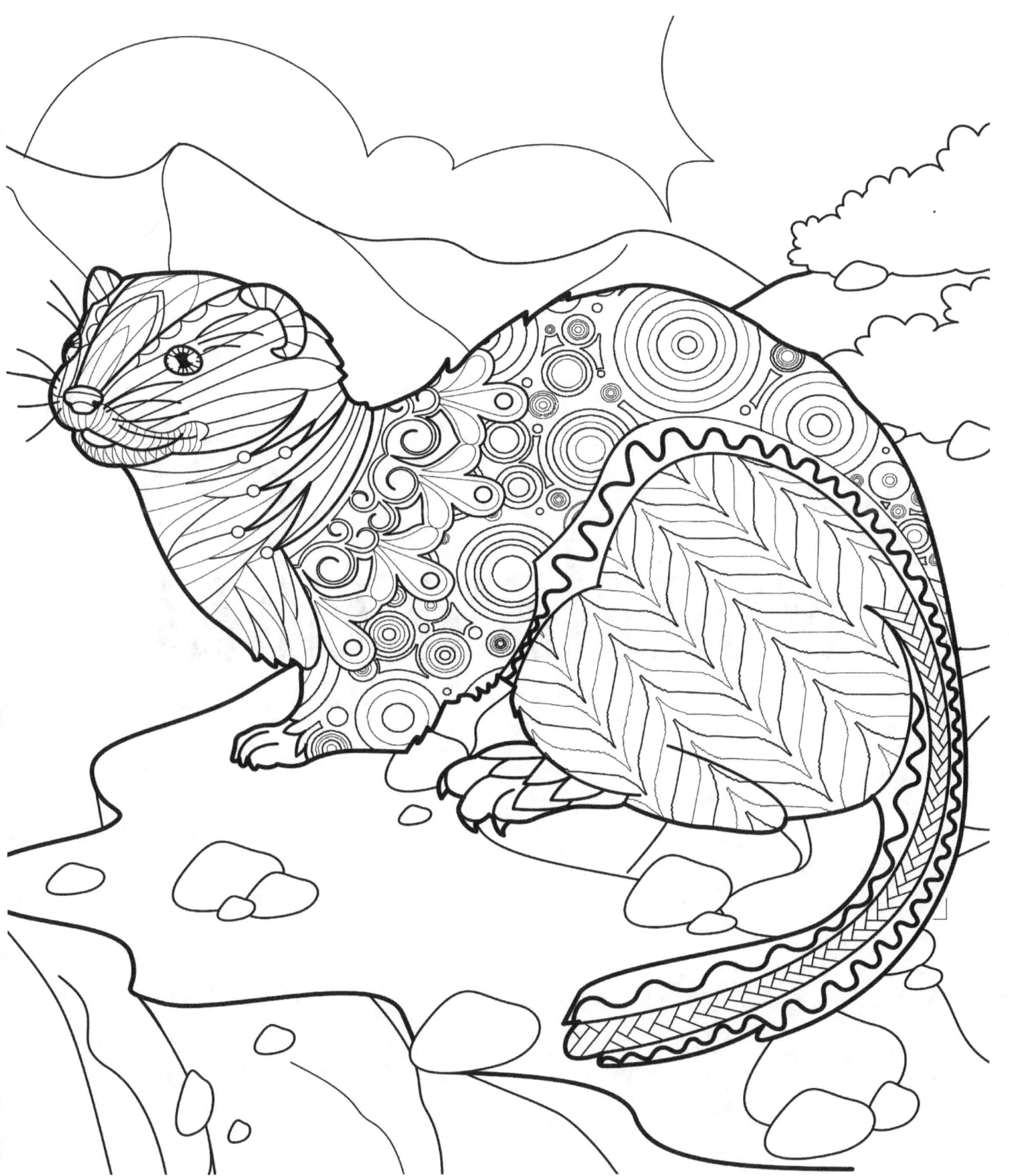

Mountain Goat

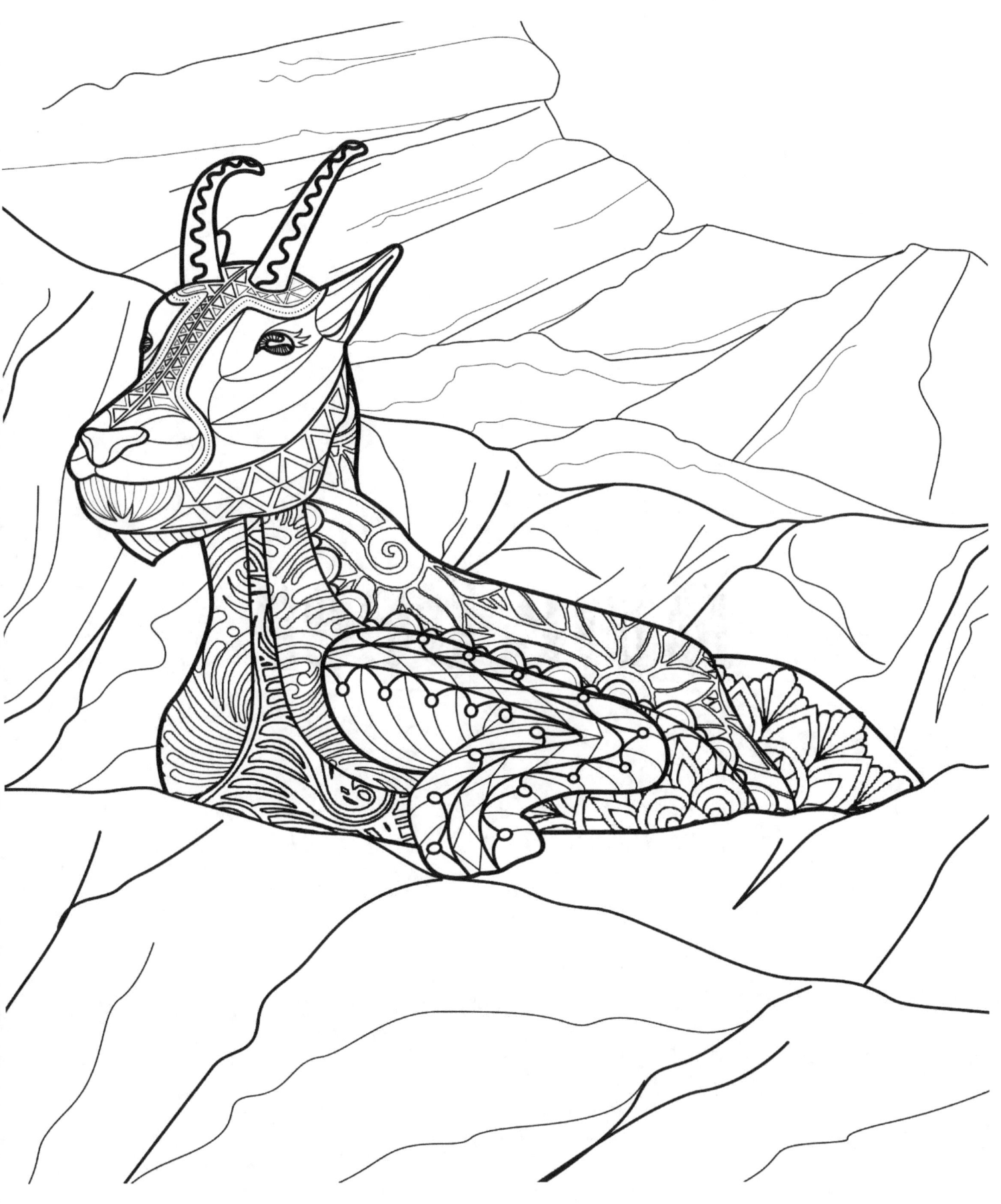

Mule Deer

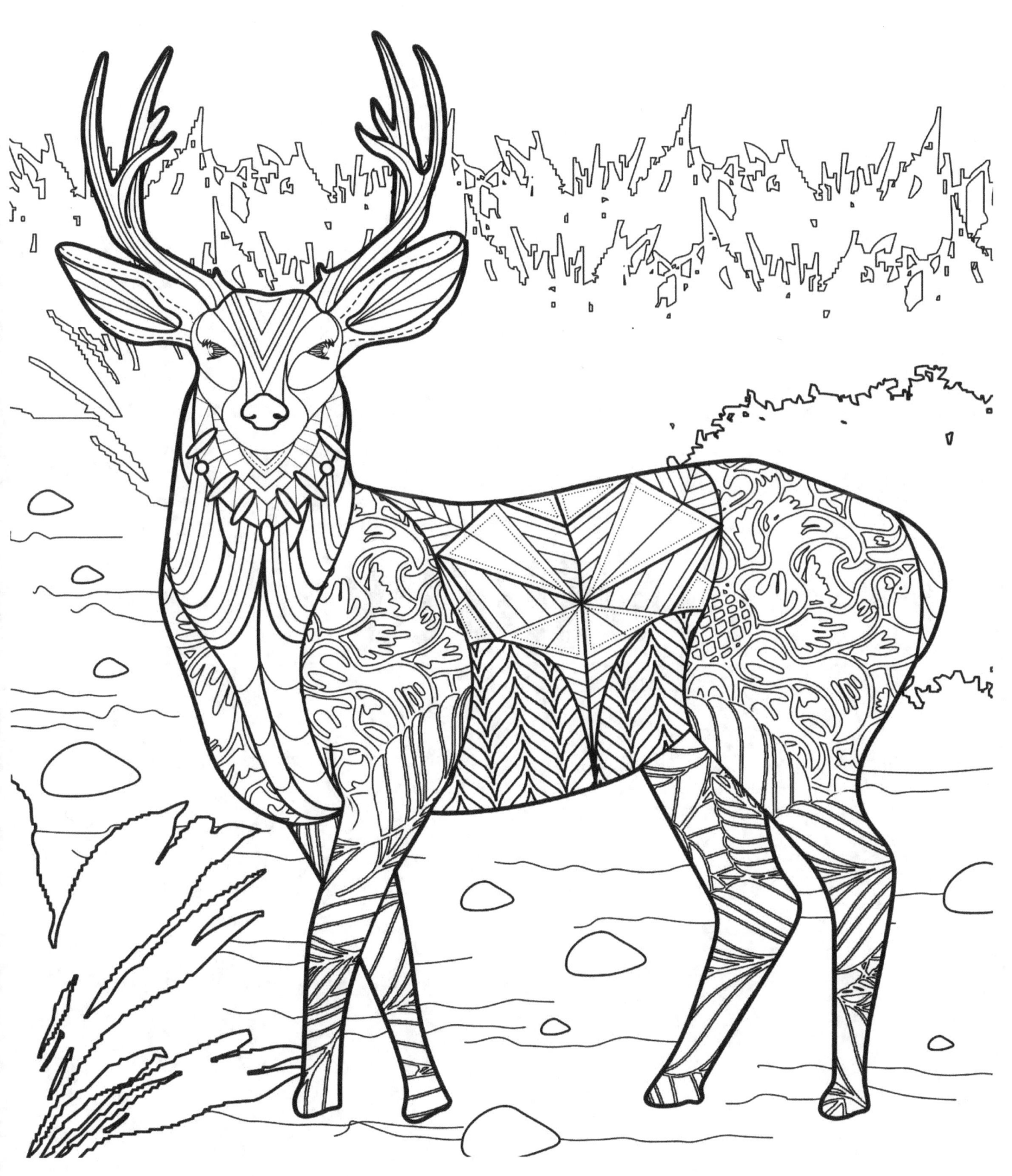

Osprey

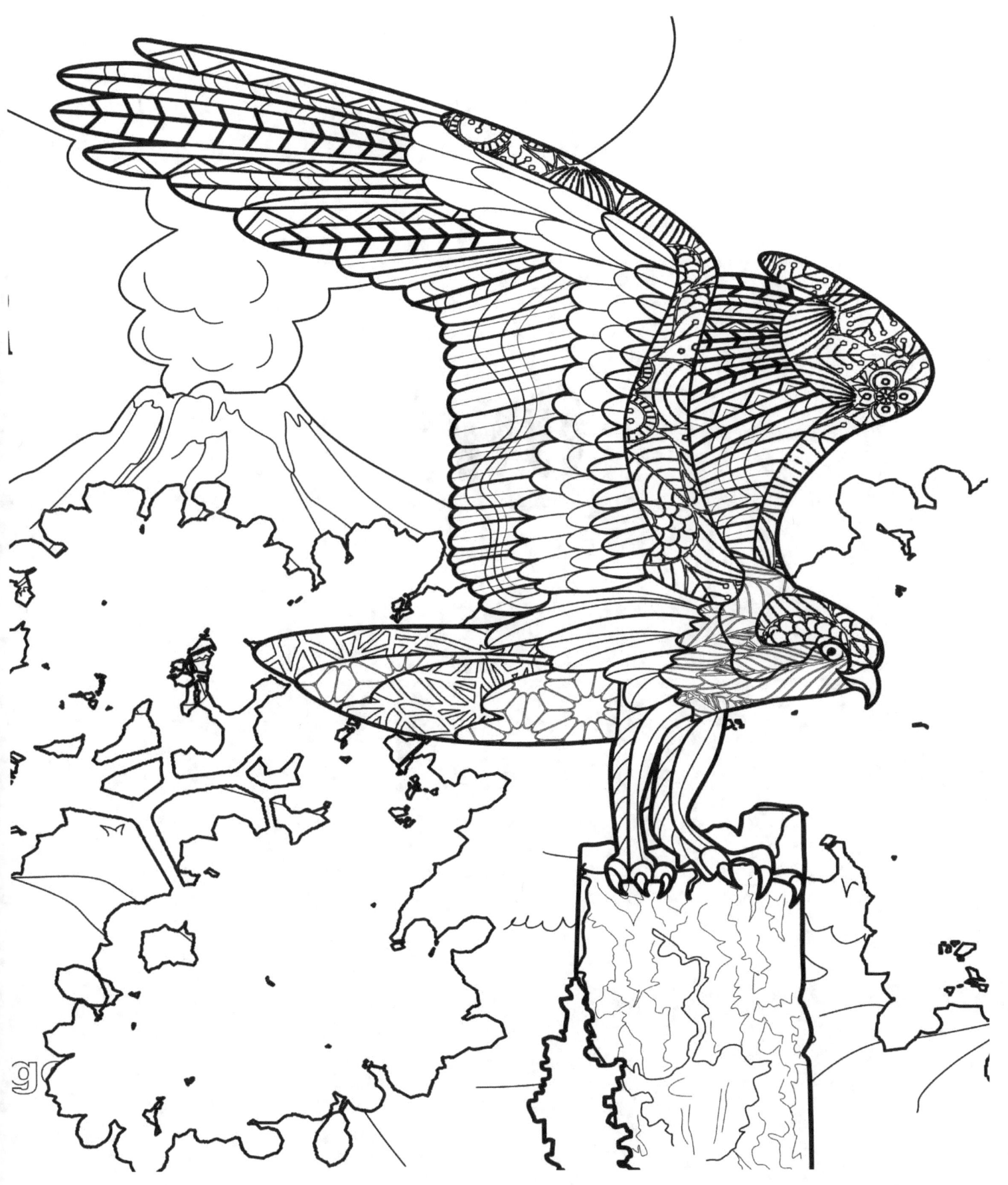

Owl

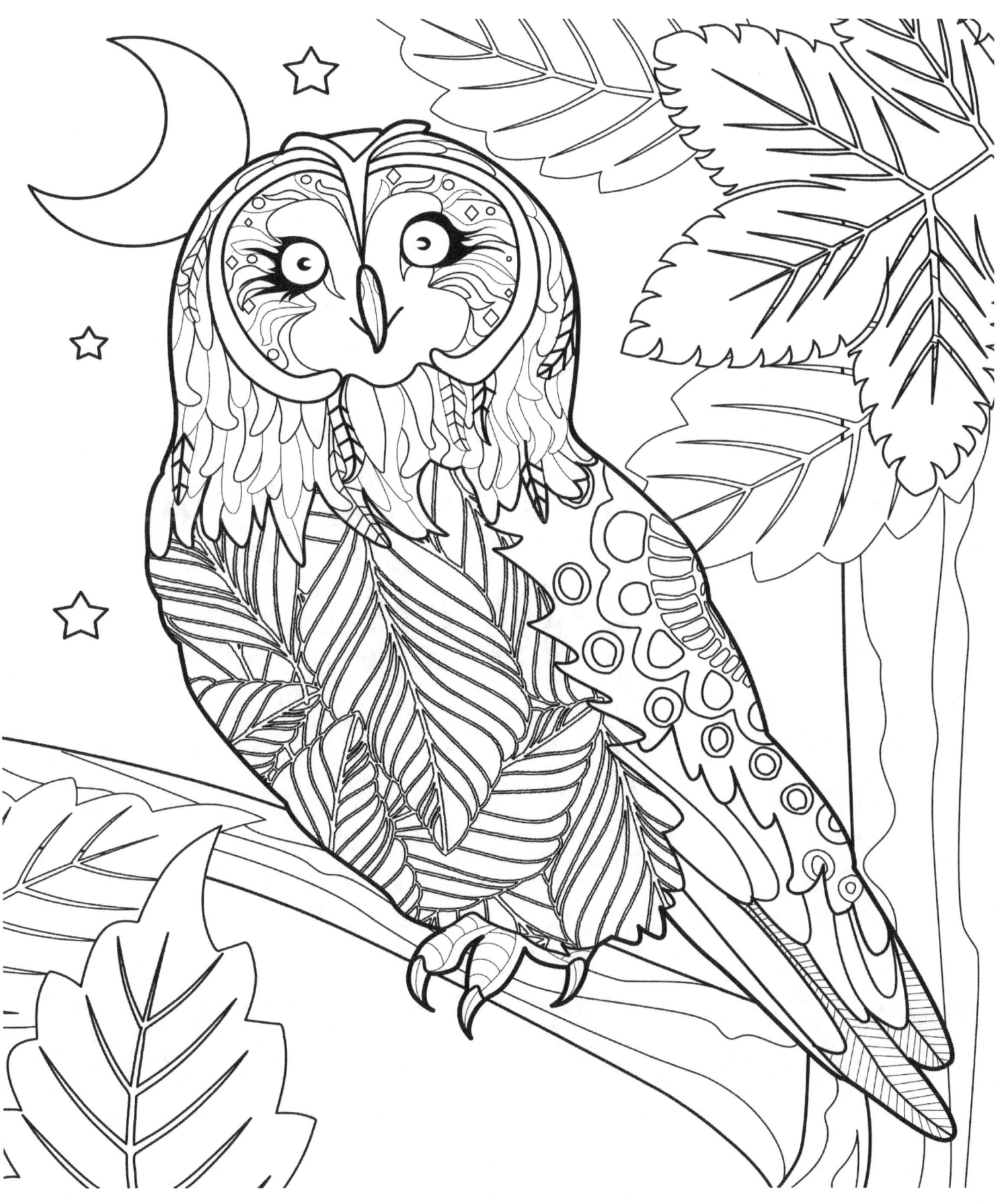

Perch

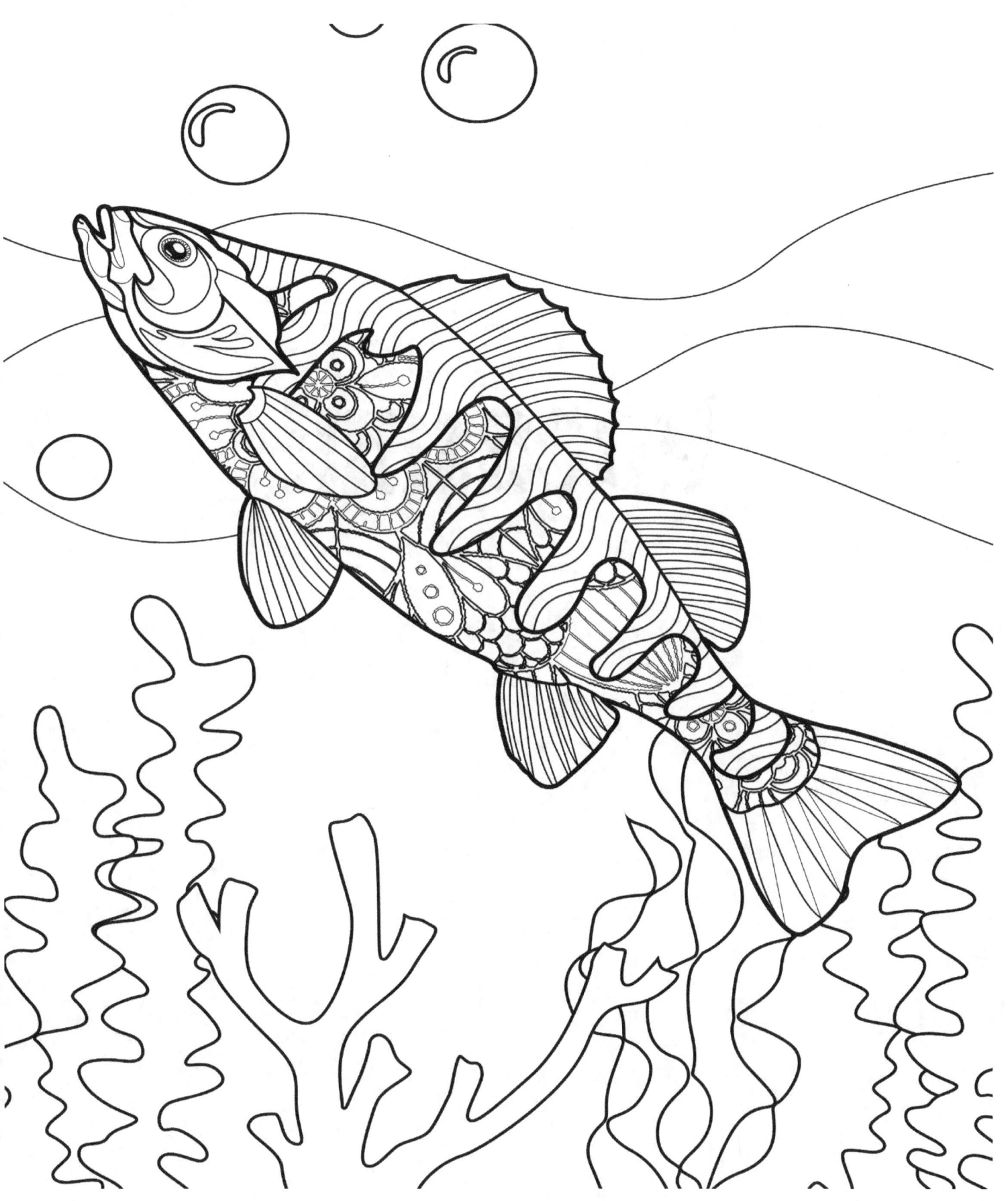

Pheasant

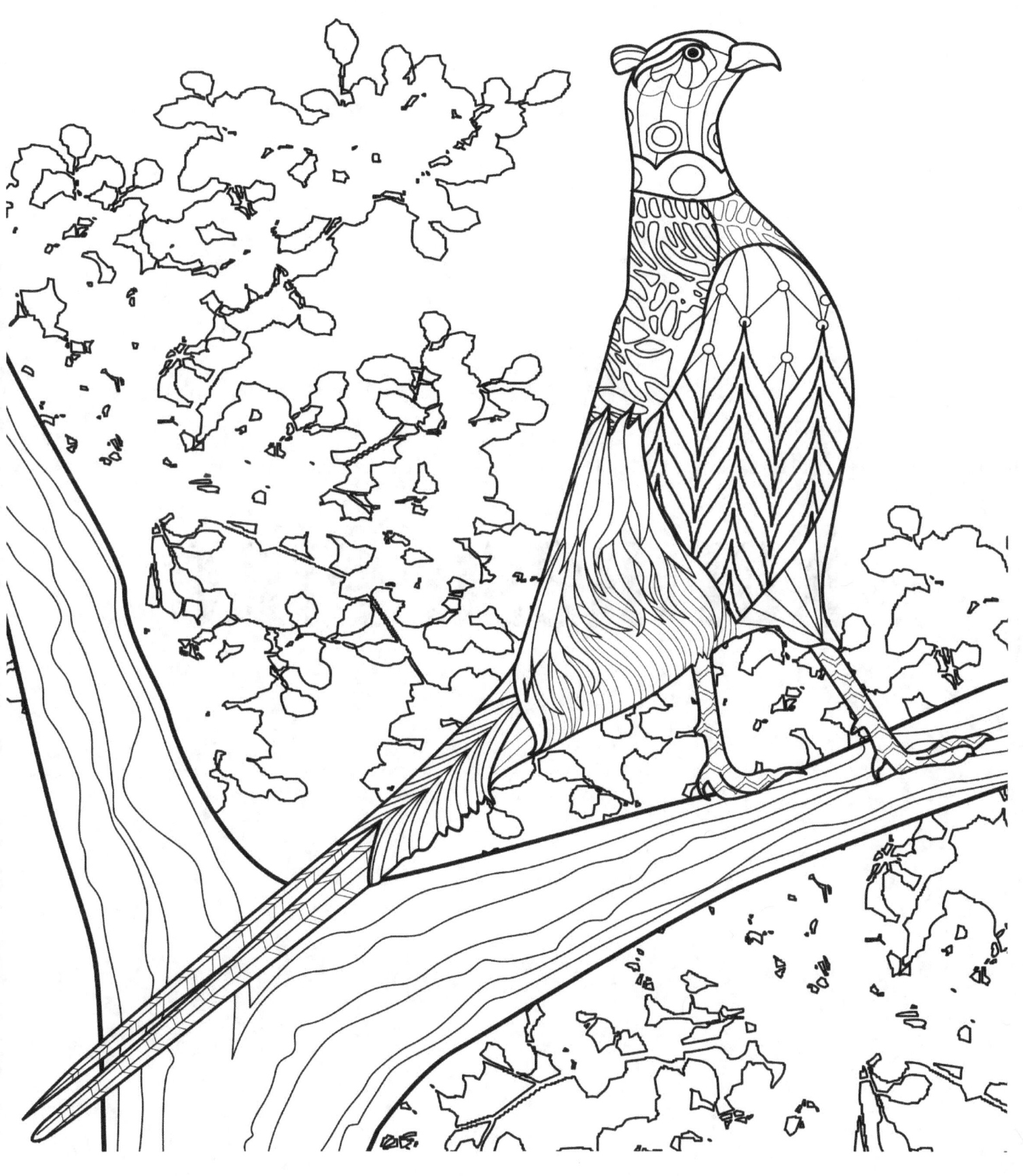

Northern Pike

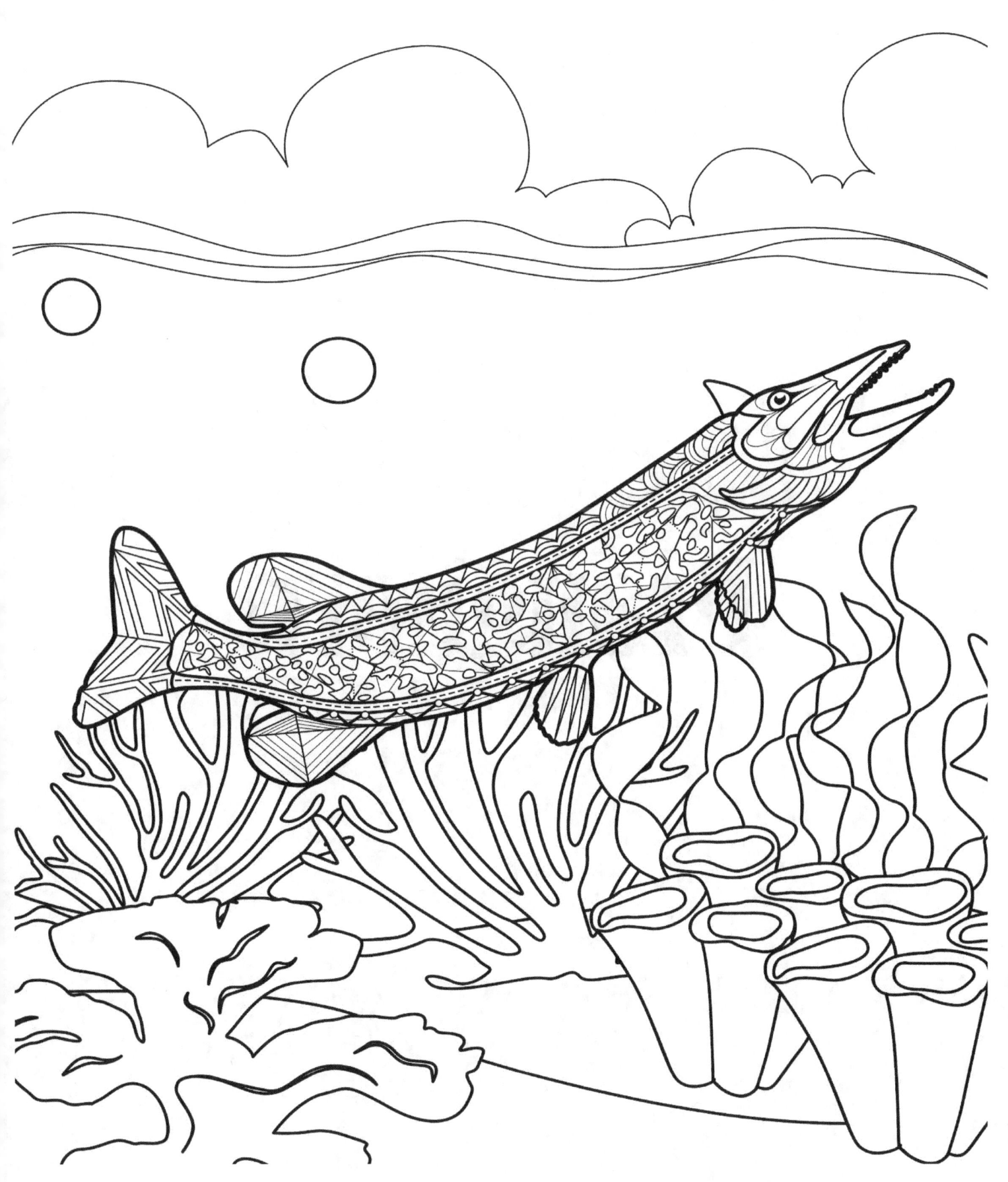

Pronghorn

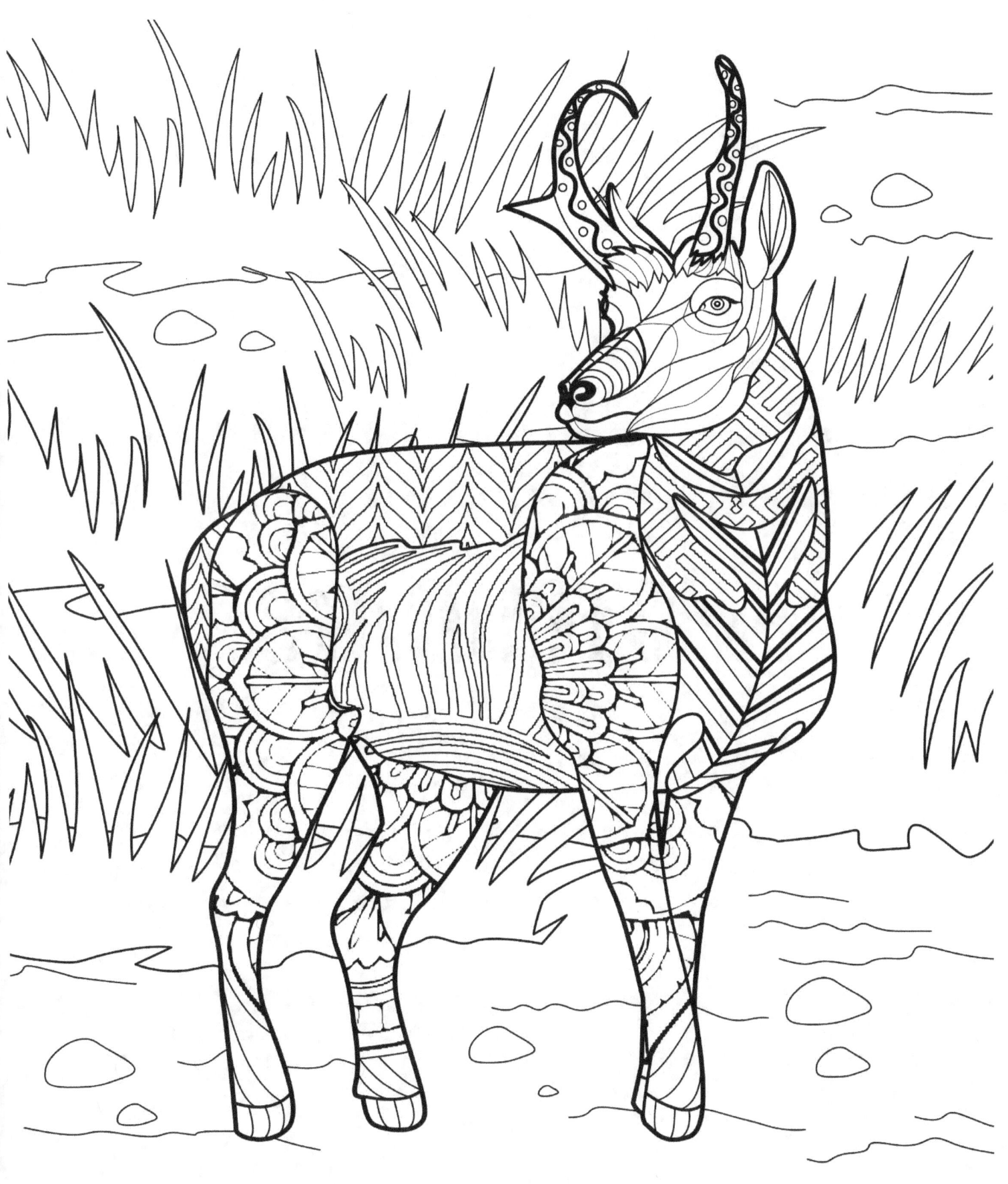

Porcupine

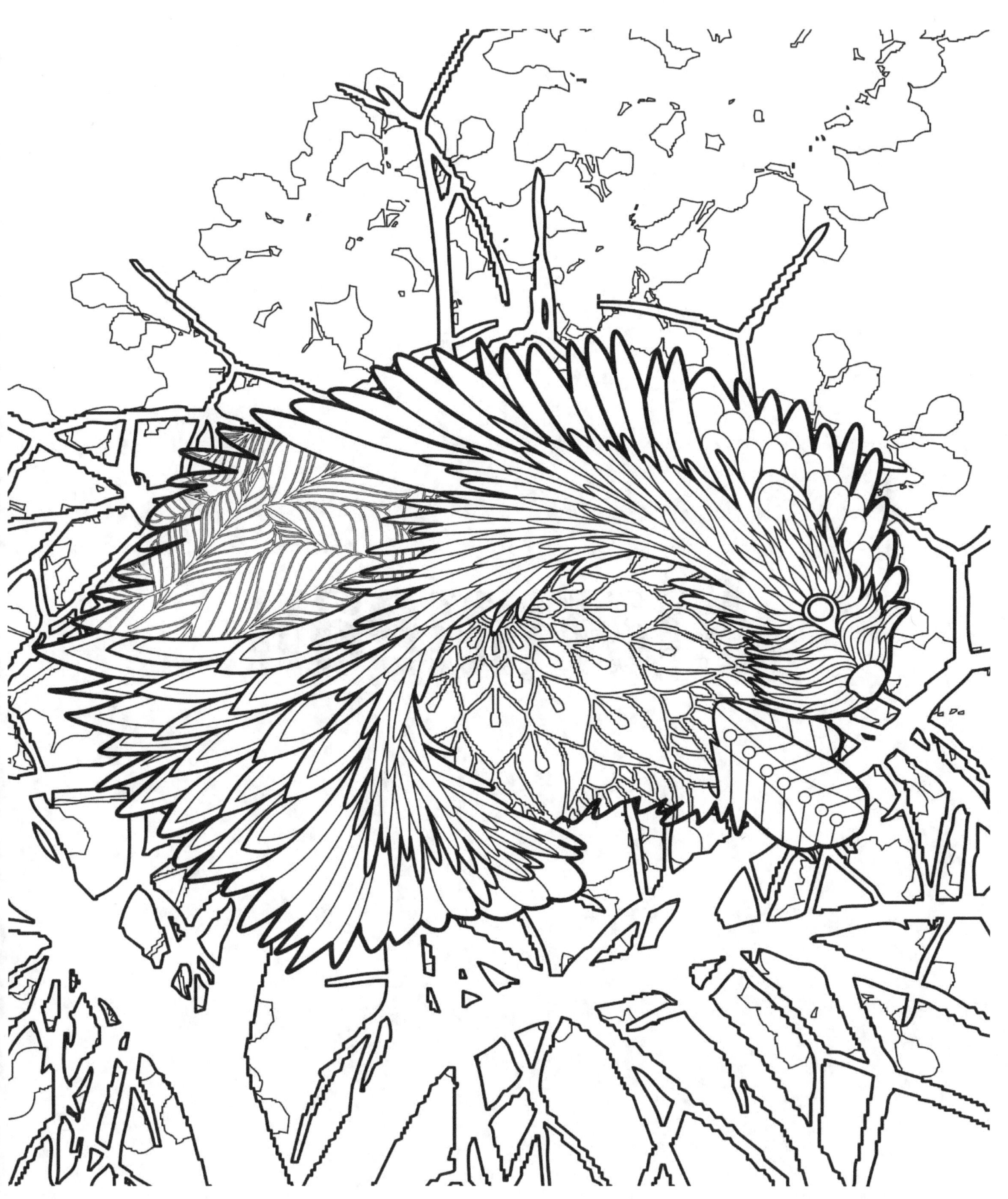

Ptarmigan

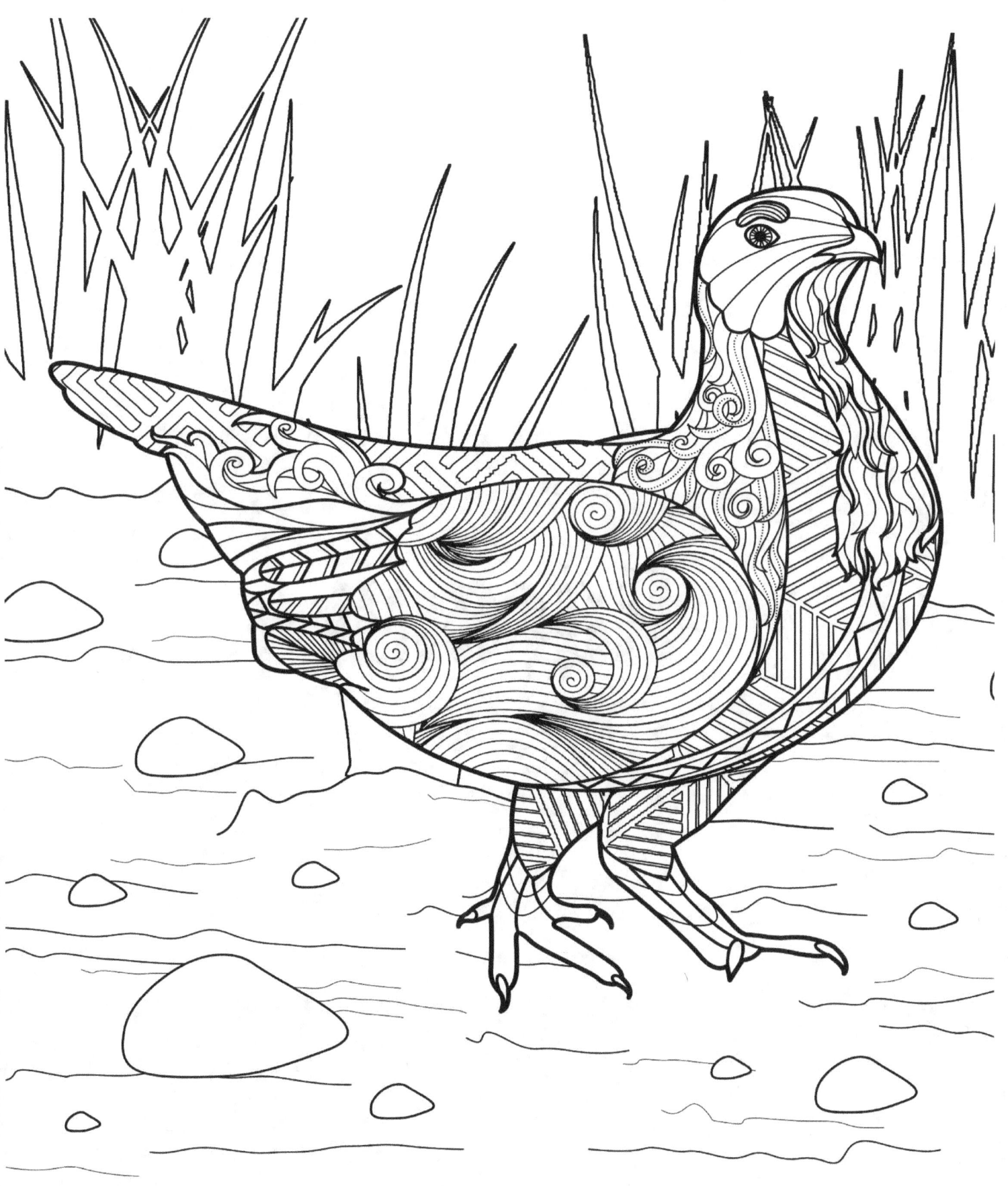

Racoon

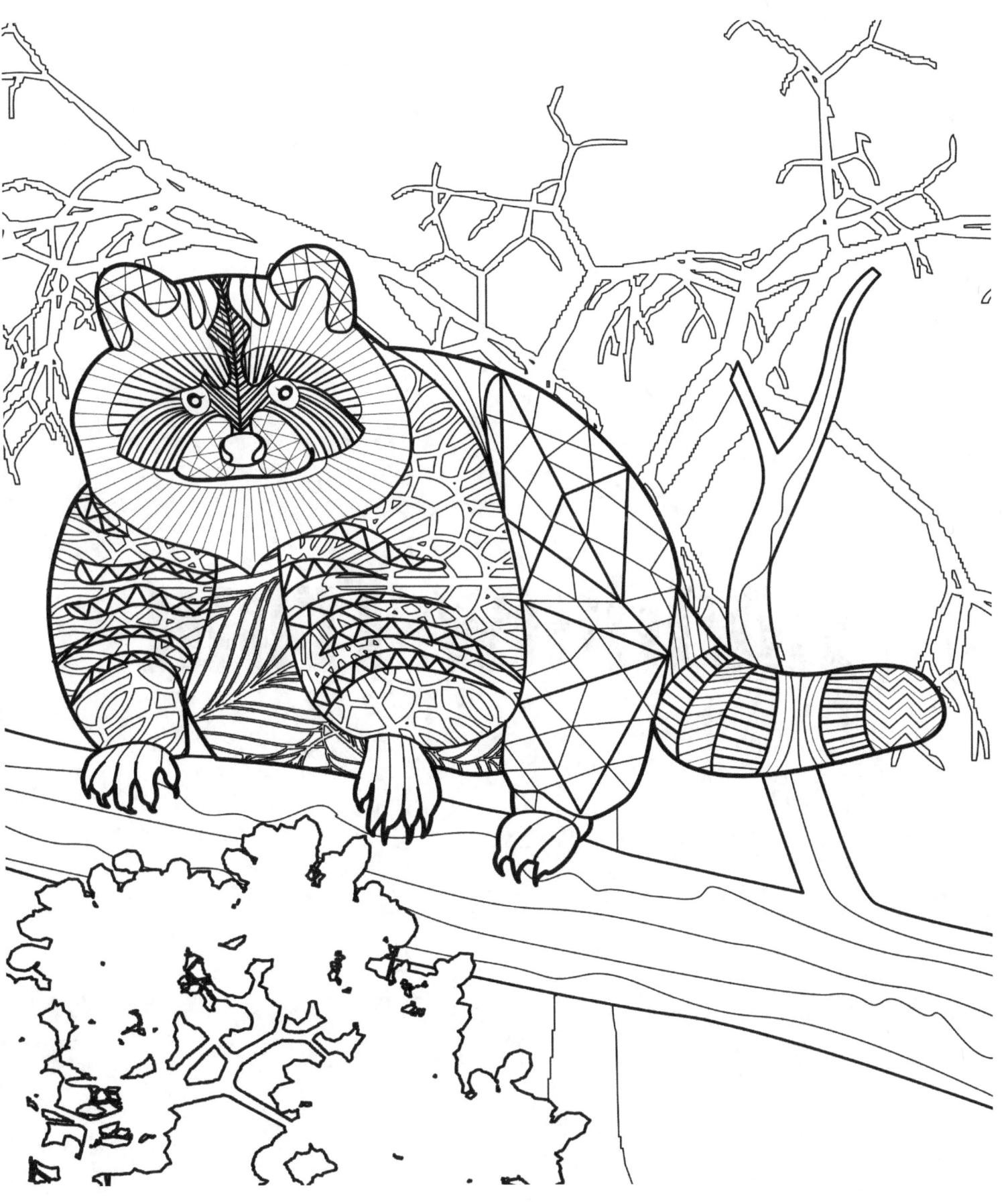

Rainbow Trout

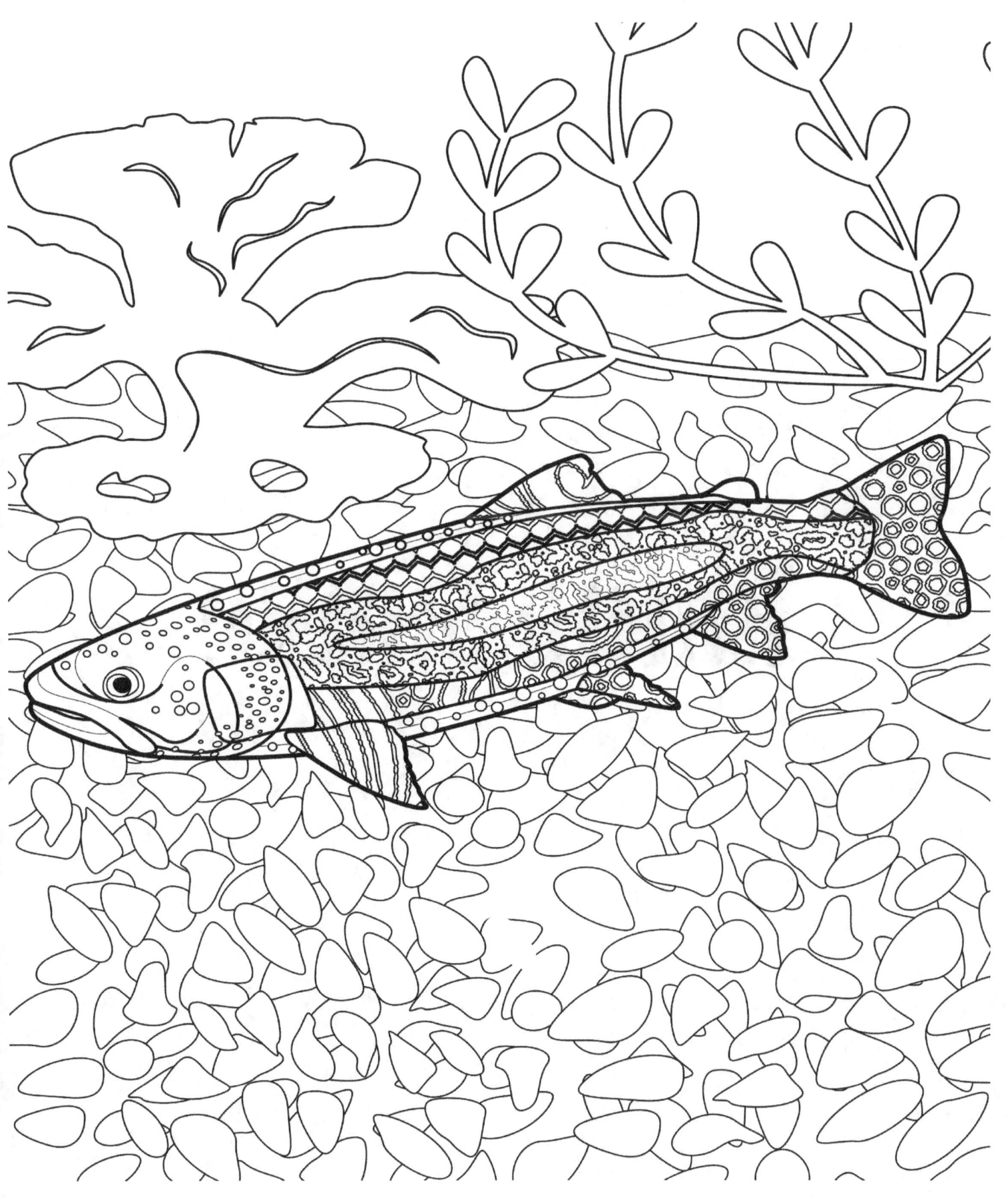

Rattle Snake

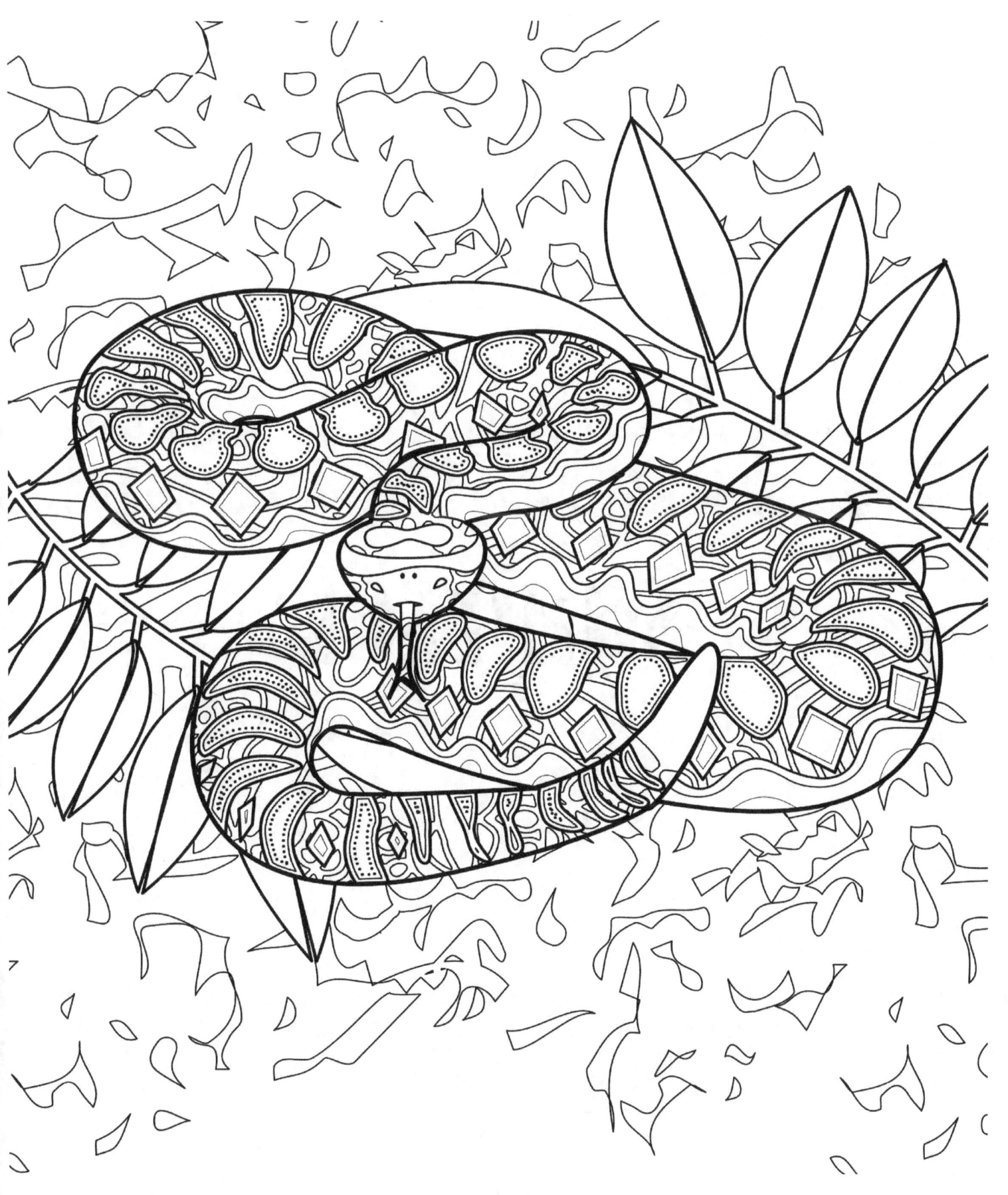

Squirrel

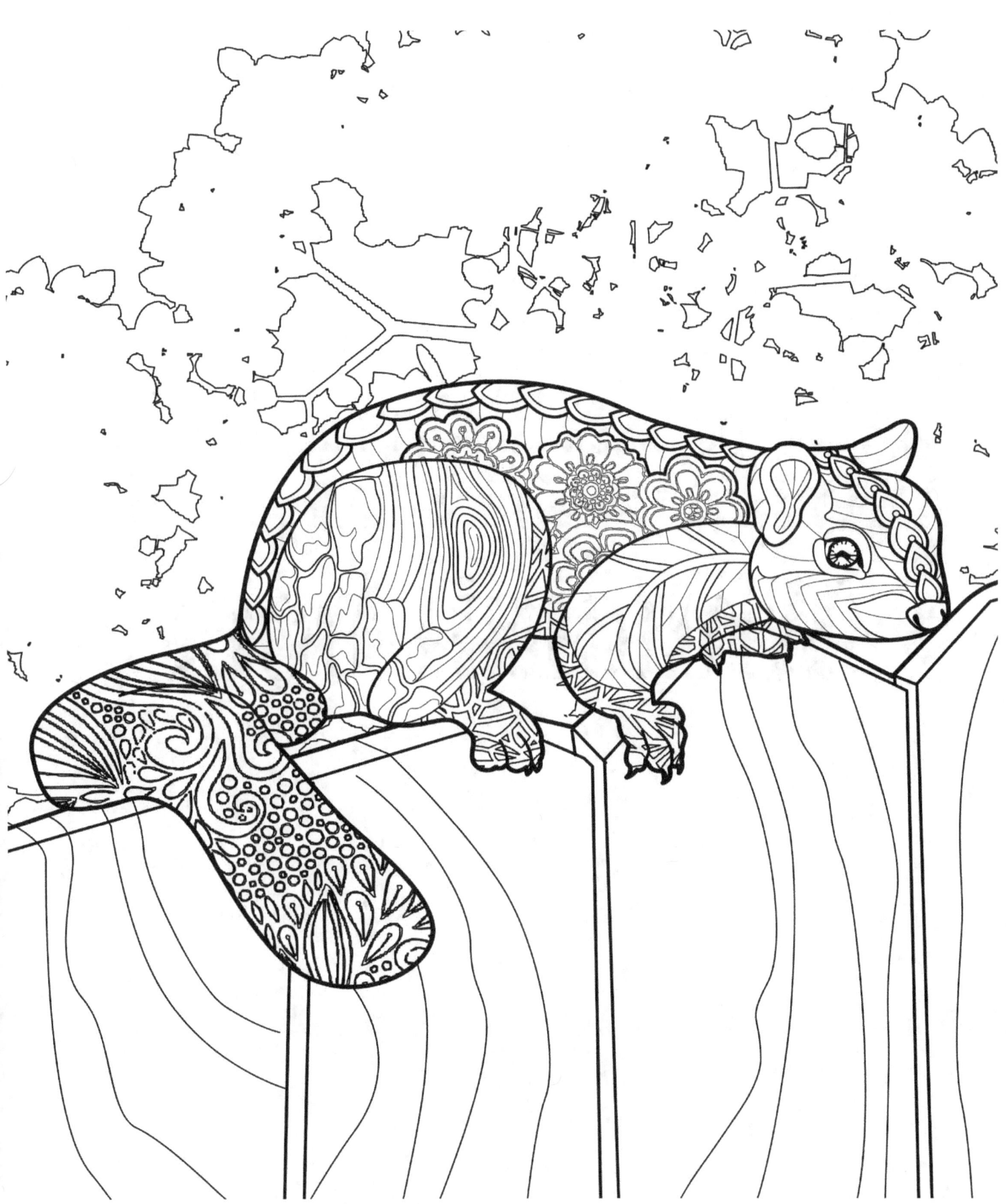

Whitetail Deer

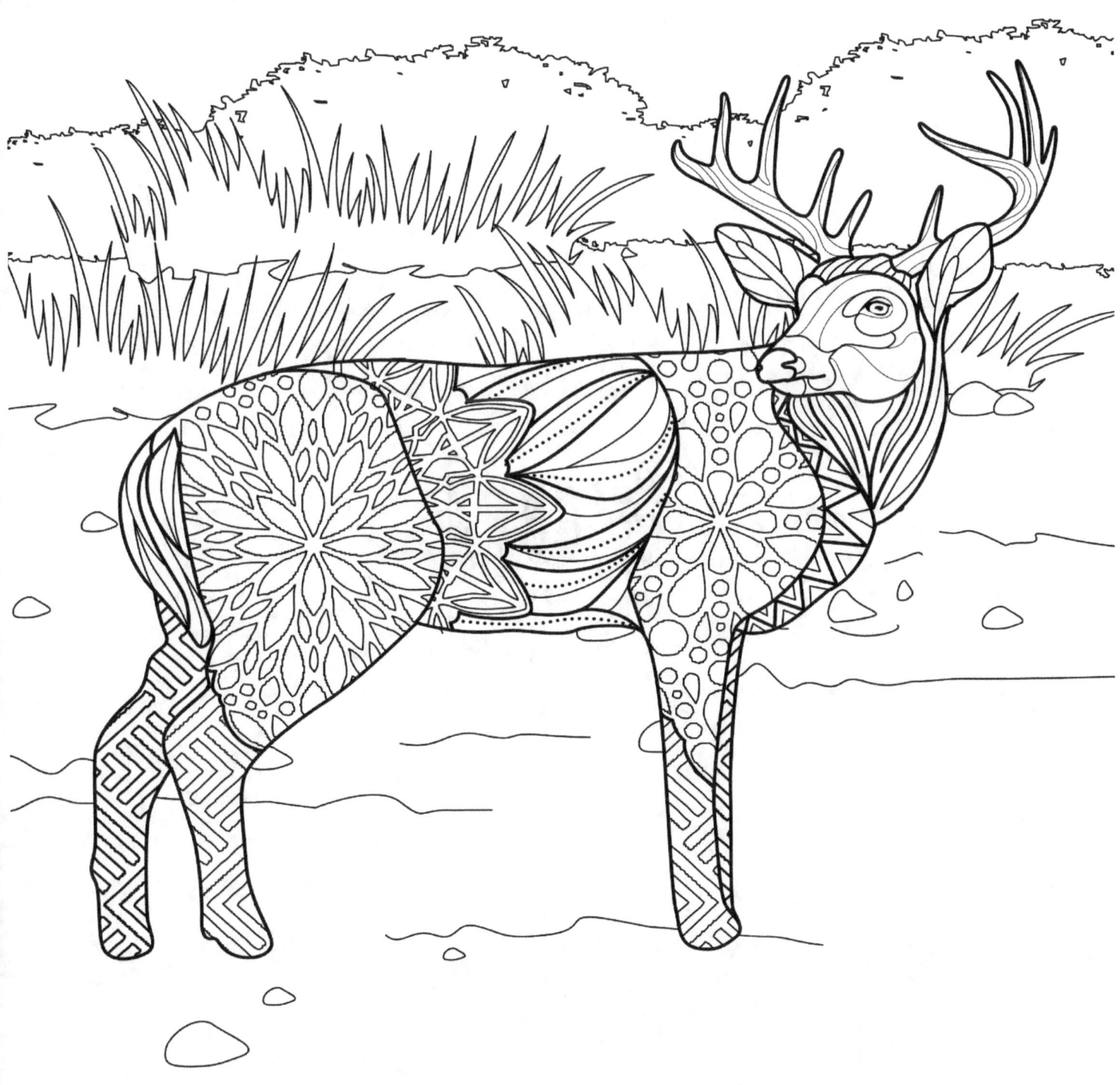

Wolf

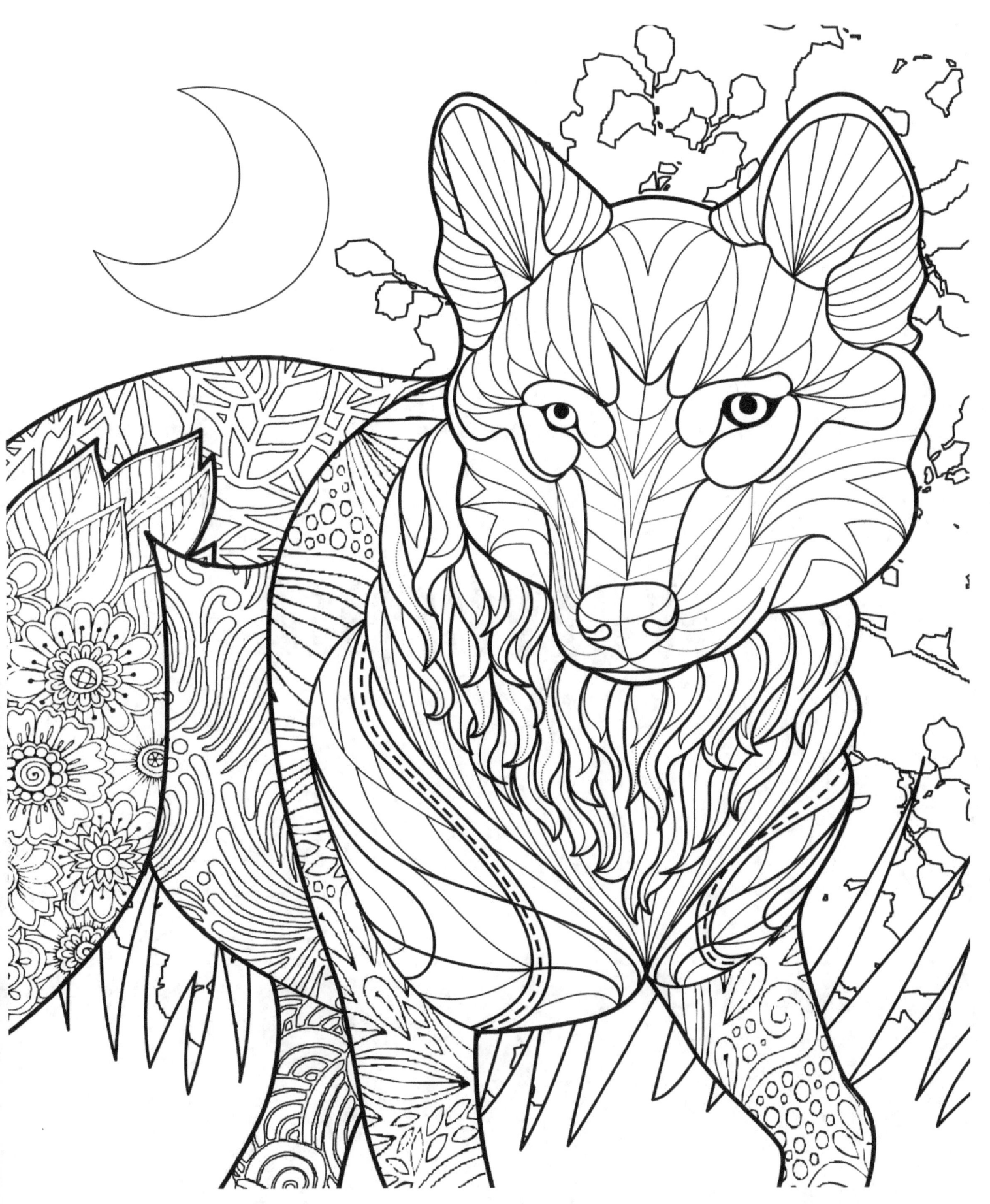

Wolverine

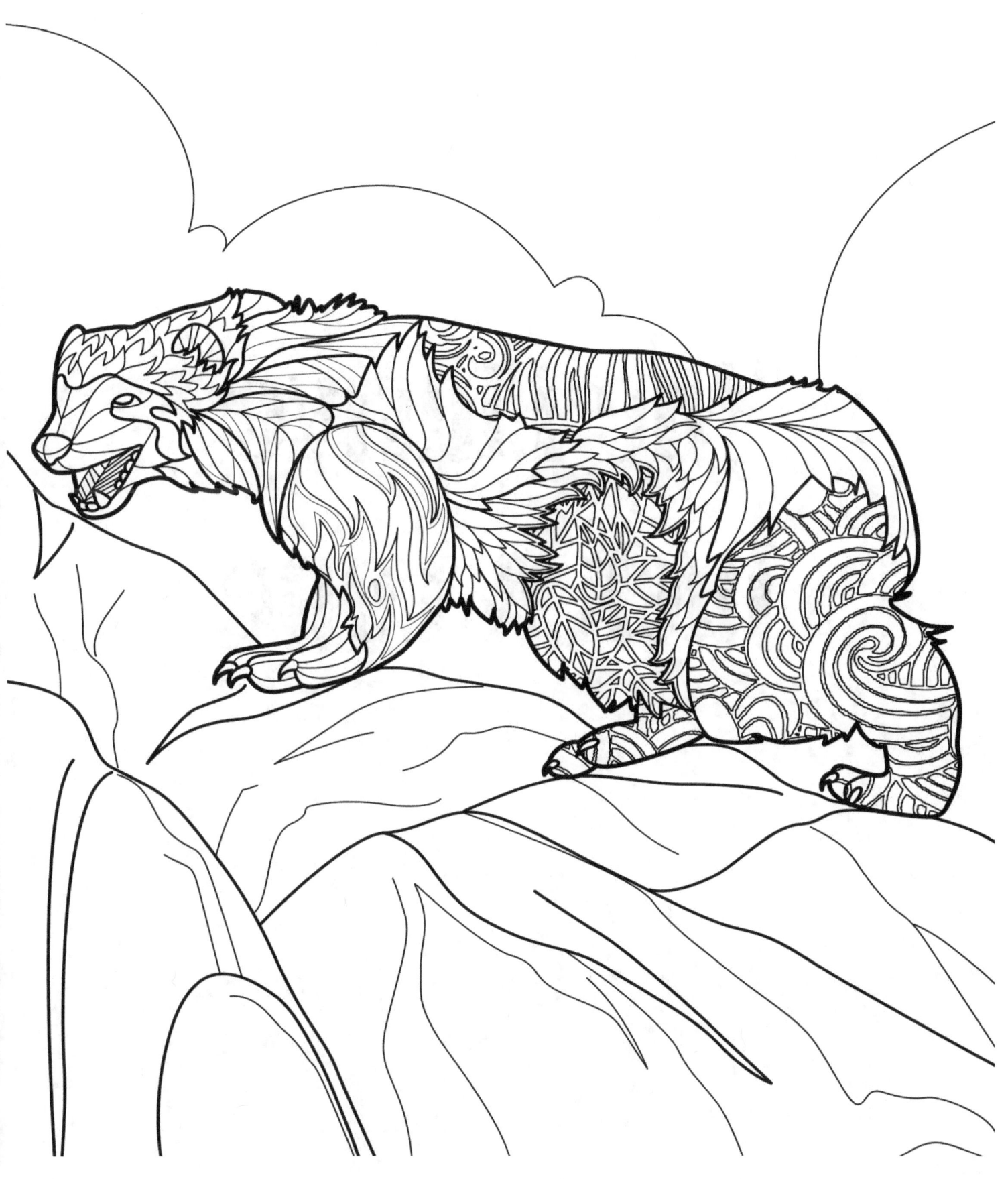

The Elusive Jack A Lope

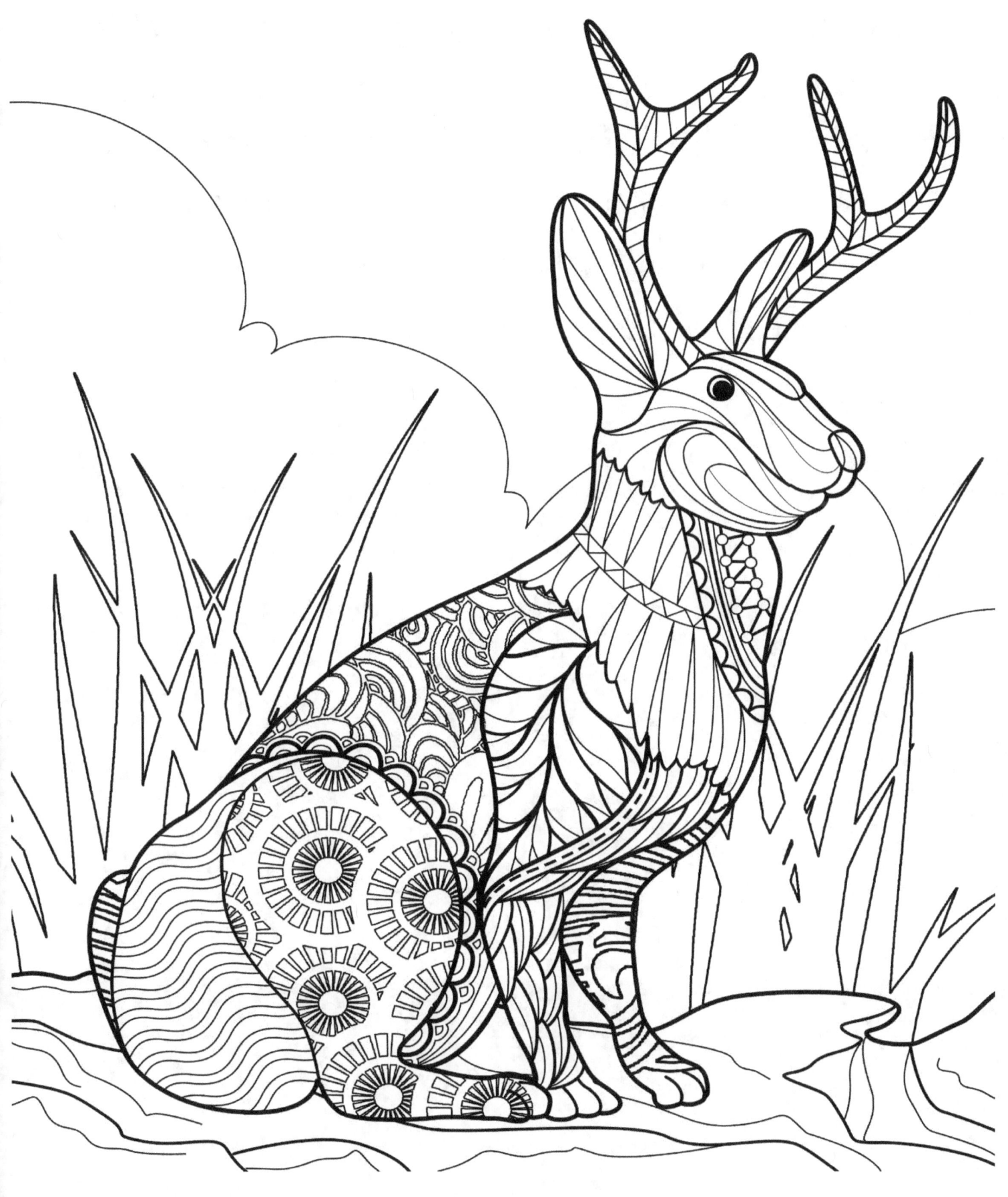

Thank you so much for purchasing this book I have put a lot of love in to this Project. I look forward to many more! If you would like to receive info on future offerings please email me at <u>monicamountainbook@gmail.com</u>

Thank You

Monica